E N D O

MW00610571

Ron Luce, whom God is using to launch a revolution in thousands (
youth, has now given youth leaders high-impact resources to birt
God's youth revolution in thousands of local churches. Pastors, hel
fire this youth revolution by buying and sending copies of this boo
to other pastors, parents of youth, youth leaders, and teachers.

Rev. Dr. Jimmy Buskir

Ron Luce has produced an easy-to-read "how-to" manual for growing a youth ministry. Moreover, it is written in an encouraging and
nurturing style that can help jump-start your youth ministry.

Joseph Tkach, D. Min, President
Worldwide Church of God

Double Vision is a great and necessary tool for youth workers. It is an
on-the-edge approach to youth ministry that can indeed revolution-
ize your group.

Dr. Jack Hayford

As a denominational official, I can't wait to get *Double Vision* in the
hands of our regional, district, and local youth leaders. It is purpose-driv-
en, passionate, and practical. Whether a veteran or novice in the high
call to rescue a lost generation of kids—this "Complete Guide for
High-Impact Ministry" will answer critical questions, give clear
direction, and dress theory in denim. Ron has hit it out-of-the-park
and over-the-wall.

Jeff Farmer, President
Open Bible Churches

The opportunities of these times call for dedicated youth leaders who
will mobilize youth for meaningful ministry over a lifetime. We need
youth leaders to move beyond social club ministry to equipping
leaders for God's Kingdom. Ron provides effective strategies and
essential advice for youth leaders who want to see God transform
lives.

G. Craig Williford, Ph.D, President
Denver Seminary

DOUBLE VISION

- HAVING A DREAM FOR HIGH IMPACT YOUTH MINISTRY -

RON LUCE

Double Vision — Having a Dream for High Impact Youth Ministry
Published by TM Publishing, a division of Teen Mania Ministries
22392 FM 16 West Garden Valley, TX 75771
www.teenmania.org

ISBN 978-1-936417-03-2
© 2010 Ron Luce

Printed in the United States of America

RELIGION / CHRISTIAN MINISTRY / YOUTH

DEDICATION

This book is dedicated to those who
have poured their guts out for this
generation.

ACKNOWLEDGMENTS

The Double Vision book series is the effort of many people's time and energy. I would like to acknowledge a few of those individuals.

Thank you to my Executive Team, Beth Powell, Rebekah Morris, Emily Johnson, Heidi Abigt, Laurie Fields, and LauRen Spillers. Thank you for all the work you do to keep things flowing and for all the hours that you put into making this book possible.

This book series would be meaningless without all the Youth Pastors and Youth Workers in the world. If you are a Youth Pastor or Youth Worker, I want to thank you for the time, blood, sweat, tears, and pizza you have gone through to reach this generation.

I have to acknowledge my amazing children Hannah, Charity, and Cameron. My wife of over 25 years, Katie, you are a wonderful wife, mother, and best friend.

Finally, John 15:5 says, *"I am the vine, you are the branches. . . without Me you can do nothing"* (NKJV). My life is nothing without the Lord. There aren't enough words in all the books in all the world to express how thankful I am to You.

CONTENTS

Dear Youth Leader,

We are in the middle of a battle for the hearts of a whole generation. If you are like most youth leaders in America, you are in the trenches every day. You're wearing yourself out trying to do whatever you can to love kids, lead them to Christ, and help them grow. Even with all that's done in the name of youth ministry, we are still losing a generation. It seems like the media and the enemy have been working harder than we have. They are destroying a generation at a faster rate than we are rescuing it. At current rates of evangelism, only four percent of this generation will be Bible-believing Christian adults. If we continue doing youth ministry the way we have been, we will end up with an America unlike any we have ever known. Something has to change!

What you have in your hands is more than a book series. This is a manual to provoke a revolution in communities, churches, and youth ministries across America. If we want to capture the heart of this generation before it's too late, we need thousands of youth ministries and groups to double and disciple every year. *Double Vision* will help you to build a thriving, solid youth ministry that continues to flourish and grow without burning you out.

This book series and its accompanying CD-ROM are embedded with proven strategies and principles for building a thriving youth ministry. Already, thousands of youth pastors across the country are seeing God work powerfully through these new paradigms!

I encourage you to begin to dream God's dream for you in youth ministry. Could you be one of the 100,000 youth groups needed to capture the hearts of this generation? I believe if we all throw our hearts into this, work hard, work smart, and ask the Holy Spirit to guide us, we can win this war! We need to have drastic change . . . it has to start now . . . it has to start with us.

I look forward to laboring with you and thousands of other youth pastors of every denomination and background. I believe we will see a miracle in the hearts of this generation!

Consumed by the Call,

Ron Luce

President and Founder
Teen Mania Ministries

INTRODUCTION

You have in your hands a document of war—a blueprint for strategic thinking about your local youth ministry. It is meant to help you launch a local offensive in your region to rescue teens caught in the middle of the current war for their hearts and minds. It is meant to provoke a revolution in youth ministry.

We must come to grips with the fact that—in spite of all of our best efforts to minister to young people—we are on the brink of losing a generation! The world and the enemy have been working harder, investing millions, and gaining more ground than we have. We cannot simply do more of the same old things and hope to turn this generation around. We must change what we are doing. We must change how we think about youth ministry before it is too late.

What do I mean by too late? First, consider the numbers: the millennial generation is the largest and richest generation in American history. Every year, 4.5 million American teenagers turn 20, and research shows that the odds against someone turning to Christ after reaching this milestone are significant. (We know that 77 percent of people who receive Christ do so before they are 21 years old). At the present rate of evangelism, only four percent of this generation will be Bible-believing—so we must act NOW to prevent them from going into their adult years as unbelievers.[1] Our passion is fueled by the fact that in five to seven years MOST of this generation will be in their 20s. NOW is the time to capture their hearts.

With the urgency of the moment fresh in our minds, let us approach youth ministry with a new perspective. It is time to shift our focus off of maintaining ministry the way it's always been done—the weekly meetings, our regular programs, ski trips and bake sales. What will capture the critical mass of the youth in any region is a vision-driven, not program-driven, local youth ministry. And that is where you come in!

Those of us engaged in youth ministry need to redefine our job descriptions. In this war for today's generation, we are the generals. Wars are won by the generals in the field, and those generals must have a plan to win each battle. That is what this book is all about—a new paradigm that leads to a different kind of planning and a new way of executing local youth ministry.

Don't be intimidated by the size of this book series, or get weary in the planning process. You are invited to use the text of this guide with the included CD-ROM as a tool for the battle-planning process. These steps are the work of generals that are determined to win. Let us all commit ourselves to becoming generals.

1. The Barna Group, "Research Shows that Spiritual Maturity Process Should Start at a Young Age," (November 17, 2003) ttp://www.barna.org/FlexPage.aspx?Page=BarnaUpdate&BarnaUpdateID=153

CHAPTER ONE

Raising the Standard in Youth Ministry

"What do you do?"
"I am a minister."
"Oh, you're a pastor!"
"Well, I'm just a youth pastor."

This is where our problem starts. Too many individuals involved in youth ministry today trivialize the role God has given them. Some youth leaders can barely look you in the eye when they tell you what they do. What their embarrassment communicates is, "I don't work with real people, I work with teenagers." Okay, some of you might argue that you've got teens in your group who fit in the "not fully human yet" category; nevertheless, do not underestimate

God is trusting you with the next generation of Christians.

the role God has for you in His strategy to reach today's young generation.

"Don't let anyone look down on you because you are young, but set an example for the believers in speech, in life, in love, in faith and in purity" (1 Tim. 4:12). Ever preach that passage to your students? Paul exhorts Timothy not to let anyone look down on his youthfulness, so why let people look down on those who work with youth? Youth work is not a second-class calling—it's not a holding pattern until you become a "real" pastor. This is where the action is! This is the final frontier of the future church.

Think about it! God is trusting you with the next generation of Christians. If you don't do your job, in a few years your pastor won't have a job because the number of teens entering adulthood and joining the ranks of the unchurched will continue to escalate. Whenever a friend of mine leaves youth ministry to become a "senior pastor," I always tell them how sad I am for their demotion; they are walking away from where the action is.

So I propose we redefine what it is we do. The next time someone asks you, "What do you do?" answer, "I am a Youth Specialist." When they ask what that is, confidently tell them that you "specialize in reaching people that no one else knows how to reach and many have given up on."

Youth Specialists. The title comes with some expectations. Youth Specialists are skilled practitioners in youth work. They are professionals who are committed to doing their work faithfully and with excellence. Youth Specialists are leaders with a specific area of expertise that is of value to others. Youth Specialists are trained to do what no one else can do.

HOW WE GOT HERE

Many of us got into youth ministry when we heard our pastor say, "Brother Dave, could you help out for a little while with the young people? We're between youth pastors, and we need a volunteer for just a month or two, until we get back on our feet."

Five years later, you're frantically filling balloons with whipped cream in preparation for another meeting, and you're running late. You still have to hop in the church van to pick up the "outlying" members. But first . . . mop up the soda spill from last week . . . arrange those chairs . . . and . . . I honor you. You saw the need; you chose to act.

Now you've been working with kids for years. You love it but you still feel less than qualified. True, there's a noble, positive side to this scenario. Thank God you are using your time and energy to touch lives. And God, by His marvelous grace, definitely uses the willing, whether you're qualified or not: "For the foolishness of God is wiser than man's wisdom, and the weakness of God is stronger than man's strength" (1 Cor. 1:25).

You may also be thinking, "Well, I know this ministry isn't all that great or organized but it's better than what the kids had before. The guy they had before just left them. It's way better than nothing." Or, "C'mon, I'm only a volunteer. What do you expect?"

If you are called to youth ministry, you are called to something that's worth doing right.

Here's my point: Whether you are a volunteer, a paid staffer, or a regular helper, if you are called to youth ministry, you are called to something that's worth doing right. For too long youth ministry has been languishing at the bottom of the totem pole. As a result, our image and performance have suffered. Since others don't treat us as if we are important, we begin to believe that we're not very important. Then we don't treat the students as if they are very important. Yet, how important is our Boss? Doesn't He deserve better?

GOD IS WORTHY OF...WHAT?

Maybe we need to back up a bit and ask ourselves: Why is the world doing things in a world-class way, while God's people are always playing catch-up? God's model for doing things—from Creation to Incarnation to Resurrection —is extraordinary, yet we settle for average. Christians need to realize that we ought to be setting the pace and defining excellence for the world instead of letting the world set the standard. Listen to the Lord Himself for a moment:

> "A son honors his father, and a servant his master. If I am a father, where is the honor due me? If I am a master, where is the respect due me?" says the LORD Almighty. "It is you, O priests, who show contempt for my name.
>
> "But you ask, 'How have we shown contempt for your name?'
>
> "You place defiled food on my altar.
>
> "But you ask, 'How have we defiled you?'
>
> "By saying that the LORD's table is contemptible. When you bring blind animals for sacrifice, is that not wrong? When you sacrifice crippled or diseased animals, is that not wrong? Try offering them to your governor! Would he be pleased with you? Would he accept you?" says the LORD Almighty.

"Now implore God to be gracious to us. With such offerings from your hands, will he accept you?"—says the LORD Almighty.

—Malachi 1:6–9

In Malachi's day, the law required people to bring the very best to God, the firstfruits, the thing without blemish. What has changed? Surely the basic principle remains: our God is worthy of the best.

He doesn't want our scraps.

He doesn't appreciate our odds and ends.

He isn't seeking "pretty good."

He won't be satisfied with "just okay."

No, here in the Scripture He wonders, "How dare you bring your junk to me?" Yet, in youth ministry, we become quite comfortable with not having our messages prepared before the kids come. We're okay with our youth room not being put together and our Xerox copies being hard to read. We excuse away lots of little things—lots of little blemishes—things that God notices. But if we keep letting a few blemishes slip by, we'll soon be letting the whole infected hippo waddle in.

No more thinking, "It's just youth ministry. We don't have a budget for it, and it's better than what the last guy did. I'm just trying to help these kids!" Yes, we need to do all that and help the young people. But if it is worth doing for God, it is worth doing well.

No more thinking, "It's just youth ministry. We don't have a budget for it, and it's better than what the last guy did."

"And you say, 'What a burden!' and you sniff at it con-temptuously," says the LORD Almighty.

"When you bring injured, crippled or diseased animals and offer them as sacrifices, should I accept them from your hands?" says the LORD.

—Malachi 1:13

Like the people of old, we're tempted to moan, "It's just too hard!" And it is hard, because . . .

we don't have money;
we don't have a budget;
we don't have the time;
we don't have a staff;
we don't have a secretary;
we don't have a salary;
we don't have the parents;
we don't have the kids.

So much we don't have. All we have is the Almighty.

I recently visited Disney World with my family, and I noticed how it resonates with excellence. Everywhere you go, everywhere you look—you can feel it. I thought of Dr. David Yonggi Cho, the great Korean pastor, and his Disney experience. As he walked down Main Street with his American hosts, he began weeping uncontrollably. Someone asked, "Dr. Cho, why are you crying? Most people come to Disney World and get happy."

"Why does the world emphasize excellence so much?" he replied. "Yet we Christians just give God our leftovers."

For the sake of money—for a dream, for a wildly imaginative piece of fantasy—people will work hard to create a work of excellence, with not a gum wrapper lying on the ground.

Full-time or paid staffer or volunteer. If we are called

to do youth ministry, it is worth doing with excellence. Excellence is important because:

Excellence melts young hearts. At an event with 60,000 kids in the Pontiac Silverdome, I was speaking with an 18-year-old young lady who was a believer but had back-slidden. Before the program even started, her heart was turned. How? Walking into an awesome, perfectly excellent stadium, "I felt so loved and cared for," she said. "Just to think that there are adults who would care about me and my generation so much—to provide all of this!"

Tears streamed down her face.

She hadn't even heard a preacher yet.

There is profound, persuasive power in anything that's excellent. Maybe it's because when we pursue excellence, we are tapping into the transcendent, which ultimately finds its source in God.

Look again at your calling to youth ministry. Were you called to provide a bunch of clean activities for kids? Were you called to be a Christian babysitter, to merely make sure the teens don't get into trouble, don't get pregnant, don't do drugs before they graduate?

I think not. You are called to capture young hearts for the kingdom.

Excellence makes everybody feel important. Think about it. In the midst of excellence, don't you feel kind of, well, excellent? At the end of that event in Pontiac, the man who oversees all Silverdome operations called our chief sound-and-light manager into his office. This top-flight executive sat our manager down and showed him dozens of pictures of our event.

Every aspect of our program, day by day, was there in full color for our manager to see. As our guy sat wondering what was coming, this Silverdome head honcho

Were you called to be a Christian babysitter, to merely make sure the teens don't get into trouble, don't get pregnant, don't do drugs before they graduate? I think not. You are called to capture young hearts for the kingdom.

said, "In all the years I've been running this venue, I've never seen a production this excellent. We've had every rock-and-roll group you can imagine, every kind of production with sound and light. But I've never seen anything like this. Would you be willing to let us rent your equipment and your people? Could you come in and run other productions for us in this building?"

Isn't that the way it should be? I know, it's an amazing reversal, but isn't it time that the world looked at the church and said, "I want what you've got!"?

Excellence makes victory plausible. One of the most pressing reasons for demanding excellence of ourselves is that we are right in the middle of an explosion of teenagers.

Here's what I mean. Right now about 33 million teenagers live in the U.S., up from about 27 million just a few years ago. In the next few years, the number will swell to 35 million.[1] The world is ready for this explosion. They are marketing potato chips, shoes, video games, cars, clothes—everything you can imagine—directly to these kids because they know "if we can get them to buy when they're young, they'll buy for the rest of their lives." We're talking a hundred billion dollars a year spent by teenagers.[2] Product marketers know they have to do whatever they can to snag these spenders and hold on tight.

The implications for the church? If we remember that about 77 percent of those who come to Christ do so before the age of 21, we'll recognize the critical importance of our job.[3] The world is going after them for rap music and low-riding jeans. Are we seeking them just as passionately for the Lord?

ARE YOU READY FOR THE EXPLOSION?

Ready or not, the explosion is happening. So, the question is, "Are you ready for this explosion?" You'll need to prepare in at least three major ways:

1. Make a crucial change—from minding to multiplying. We need to change our mind-set. Many of us entered youth ministry when the pastor called us up: "Our congregation is full of adults and these adults have kids. Could you do something to help keep the youth busy?" Sound familiar?

Maybe this was just God's way of getting your attention. What He really wants is someone to love all the teens in your region, so He used your pastor and the need in your church to get you started. God wants to reach kids through you, and not just the kids of your church's pew-dwellers, but all of the teens in your community! Now is the time to step into all that He had in mind when you got that first phone call.

God is trusting you with an unprecedented explosion of young people. So say farewell to the old way of thinking and tear down your boxes. You need to double and disciple for the next five years.

Isn't it time that the world looked at the church and said, "I want what you've got!"?

If your youth group has 30 teens today, next year it needs to have 60. Just think, in five years you will be impacting 480 young people on a weekly basis! And beyond just showing up on Wednesday night, each of these young people will be growing into true disciples.

Think kingdom big! It is not our job merely to mind the store.

2. Set a lofty goal—from local to global. We know we're called to reach a generation in a world-class way, a generation that is now united around the globe by a common youth culture. Demographic researchers have discovered that the bedrooms of teenagers around the world look virtually the same. Posters of the same rock-and-roll and sports stars, the same computer games, and the same MP3 downloads. Yes, MTV and its counterparts have created a global youth culture. While this is scary, it's got a powerful upside. We have a ready-made superhighway for taking the Gospel throughout the world. Cultural barriers that once posed massive communication problems are now less daunting. We're not limited by the walls of our church or even the borders of our nation. We can think globally from day one in our youth ministry.

3. Redefine a job description—from meeting-making to people-making. Now is the time to decide what's driving us. Have we set out to produce programs or disciples? Do we ask ourselves, "What are we going to do this week?" Or do we frequently stop and think, "What do we want the product of this ministry to be?"

I believe our job description is to equip teens to be like the biblical David. When he was a teenager, he killed a bear, killed a lion, and—at 17 years old—he killed the biggest (literally) enemy of his people. Our job is not just to keep people in church or to decide what games to play during Friday night's lock-in. Our job is to train up more Davids.

Our job is to encourage teens like John Mark, the teenage missionary companion to both Paul and Barnabas. He, too, was a young guy about 14 years old when he heard a knock on the door while meeting with other Christ-followers. It was Peter standing on the front porch, recently escaped from jail. A few months later, John Mark went on a mission trip with Paul and Barnabas, and later we see him hanging out with Paul. What happened to this young man as a result of constant interaction with these adult mentors? He wrote a Gospel book for our Bible! It all started while he was a teenager. Our job is to mentor teens like John Mark.

Or to build up more Timothys. The apostle Paul's young protégé was probably about 19 years old when he became a bishop, an overseer of many different churches. He discipled pastors. (Paul wrote 1 and 2 Timothy to encourage him.) Our job is to raise up more modern-day Timothys.

Are we just going to produce meetings and a fun time, or are we going to impact young men and women to be world-changers?

IT'S TIME TO STEP INTO YOUR NEW ROLE

If there's a title out there for what you do, you've heard it: youth pastor, youth guy, youth leader, youth minister, youth guide—any way you cut it, the reaction is likely the same. "Oh . . . so you're not the real pastor. You're just that guy who makes announcements on Sunday mornings."

It's time to redefine who we are and what we do. We are Youth Specialists. We are people who dedicate ourselves

Now is the time to decide what's driving us. Have we set out to produce programs or disciples?

Are we just going to produce meetings and a fun time, or are we going to impact young men and women to be world-changers?

to reaching those nobody else knows how to reach, the ones whom even the psychologists have given up on. We know that those are our kids.

The newspapers proclaim how messed up kids are, and the 10 o'clock news stresses how much trouble they make. But you, the Youth Specialist, think . . . those are my kids. You drive by a football stadium full of kids on Friday night . . . those are my kids. You see them hanging out at the mall Saturday afternoon . . . those are my kids. They don't know it yet, but they're mine!

Why are they mine? Because they are breathing, because they're in my town, and because God gave them to me. I am claiming them! I'm going to win them into the kingdom!

Now, you have to watch out if you call yourself a Youth Specialist because it is going to demand something from you.

You have to view yourself differently and behave accordingly. Why? Because there is a big difference between a "youth guy" and a Youth Specialist. Notice the contrasts:.

- **A "youth guy"** looks and acts like an overgrown teenager who's delaying his adolescence into his 30s and 40s.

- **A "youth guy"** is just kind of there. She's the young lady who's just having fun with the kids, playing Christian pin-the-tail-on-the-donkey. She's keeping the kids occupied in a clean way.

- A **"youth guy"** uses the least amount of effort to get the job done—just to keep the pastor and parents happy.

- **The Youth Specialist** concentrates on reaching young people no one else knows how to reach. It might involve a clean and fun activity, but it will definitely have a clearly defined purpose.

- **The Youth Specialist** knows the kids in her community, knows what they need, and knows exactly what she's going to do to meet those needs.

- **The Youth Specialist** faces a divine demand; he lives with his destiny. He lives with this imperative: "I absolutely must do something that impacts the young people here in a huge way. While I have breath in me, I will breathe some life into them."

When someone inquires about what you do, you know exactly how to answer: "I'm glad you asked. God has given me a vision for the young people in our city. We are building an outreach center. We're buying some buses, and we believe that by the end of the year we're going to have 500 kids with us. We are helping the kids who are _____ (name your vision). And did you know we have five girls

We are Youth Specialists. We are people who dedicate ourselves to reaching those nobody else knows how to reach.

There is a big difference between a "youth guy" and a Youth Specialist. If you specialize in touching the lives and the hearts of young people, then you are a Youth Specialist!

right now in our local high school who are pregnant and don't know what they are going to do—adopt or abort? That's not all. __ (fill in the blank) percent of the teens in our high school have parents who have divorced in the past three years."

"How do you know that?" they ask.

And you say, "What do you mean, 'How do I know that'? I get paid (or don't get paid, as the case may be) to know this stuff. I have got to know this stuff! It's my calling; it's my life. I live it; I breathe it. It's beating within me."

You pause then, letting the eye contact linger for a moment. "Maybe there's something you need to remember about me, whenever you see me around here. It's this: I specialize in touching the lives and the hearts of young people. I am a Youth Specialist."

1. US Census Bureau
2. Zollo, Peter, "The Cosmetics Category: Talking to Teens," American Demographics, November 1995, http://www.ecrm-epps.com/Expose/V3_3/V3_3_A8.asp (accessed October 25, 2005).
3. The Barna Group, "Research Shows that Spiritual Maturity Process Should Start at a Young Age," (November 17, 2003) http://www.barna.org/FlexPage.aspx?Page=BarnaUpdate&BarnaUpdateID=153

CHAPTER TWO

The 10 "Must-Haves" of a Youth Specialist

Not just anyone can call him or herself a Youth Specialist! There are some requirements to become a general in this battle for a generation. You don't have to be perfect, and you don't have to be the king of cool. But there are some imperatives.

Of course, any "youth guy" can grab a ton of resources and get by. You can go to youth leader workshops and find all kinds of curriculum, tools, magazines, videos, planning guides, and every other teen-oriented doodad imaginable. You can go to a youth pastor conference with inspiring speakers and come home fired up, but what does it change? A few weeks later, you are back to where you started.

We end up with lots of good intentions but not a lot of

We have so many ideas, but without a clear philosophy of ministry to guide us, it is unclear how to apply them all.

results. We have so many ideas, but without a clear philosophy of ministry to guide us, it is unclear how to apply them all.

Stepping into your role as a Youth Specialist is a radical mind-shift; it's a new philosophy that will dramatically impact teens in your region. But you must realize that it demands we do many things differently.

So, of all the things you could do, what are the 10 things you must do (or be)? As we explore these Youth Specialist essentials, I will ask a pointed application question with each of them. I hope you'll write your answers in the boxes provided and mull them over during the weeks and months ahead.

A YOUTH SPECIALIST . . .

. . . must have fire. Have you ever found yourself living from revival to revival, rather than living day by day with glowing coals inside? That's how our hearts ought to be—constantly glowing with the awareness of Christ's presence. We need to keep feeding that awareness so that it flames into gratitude and compassion, power and zeal.

I am not just asking if you have the fire. Notice that I'm asking, "Are you feeding it?" Look at the apostle Paul's words to young Timothy:

I constantly remember you in my prayers. Recalling your tears, I long to see you, so that I may be filled with joy. I have been reminded of your sincere faith, which

first lived in your grandmother Lois and in your mother
Eunice and, I am persuaded, now lives in you also. For
*this reason **I remind you to fan into flame the gift of***
***God**, which is in you through the laying on of my hands.*
—2 Timothy 1:3–6 *(emphasis added)*

Now think about this for a moment. Paul is writing to
Timothy, who is a leader, right? Paul had laid his hands
on Timothy, and this young man spent time with Paul,
listened to his sermons, and watched the miracles flow late
into the nights. And even he—with all his awesome advan-
tages—must keep fanning the flames?

Was Paul thinking, "Timothy, for some reason, I sense
your fire waning a little bit"? It can happen. Even if you are
a Timothy, you have to keep throwing logs on the flames of
your spiritual passion. In fact, I encourage you to quit looking like a summer barbecue pit that's gone cold.

Begin by asking yourself some tough questions:

Do I use clichés without substance?

It is easy to do. You can disguise the fact that you don't
have fire if you use clichés like, "Well, let's all praise the
Lord! Say this with me . . ."

Do I only remember the days when I was really fired up—in
the past?

But what am I like right now? So many people talk
about being on fire for God, but they are referring to yester-
day rather than to what happened in their quiet time this
morning.

How is my quiet time with the Lord?

Are you fully opening your heart to Him, dealing with

You have to keep throwing logs on the flames of your spiritual passion.

Honor should color our entire lives, characterizing who we are rather than just what we do.

the flesh, including all the areas that are kind of out of whack?

Do I tolerate compromise in my life?

Think about the times you used to say, "I would never do that!" What is excusing it now?

How can I tell if there's a fire burning inside me?

The kids can tell; they see through fake spirituality in a second. You can have great sermons and programs, but if you have no fire, you have nothing. You can only pass on what you are; your sheep will never have real spiritual fire if yours is not alive and raging out of control. A Youth Specialist MUST HAVE FIRE.

Question: *What am I doing to keep my own spiritual life burning brightly?*

. . . must have honor. Paul writes in Ephesians 4:1, "As a prisoner for the Lord, then, I urge you to live a life worthy of the calling you have received." To have this worthiness, we must live with honor. And honor calls us to look within and ask: Do I find myself excusing or justifying

small compromises? Elsewhere, the Bible says we are to avoid even the appearance of evil.

We're not just talking about the words we use when kids aren't around or the movies we rent on our day off. Honor is so much more. We cannot compartmentalize it. Honor should color our entire lives, characterizing who we are rather than just what we do.

This book will deal with honor extensively, so let me start here with just one example. Let's talk about the youth minister who comes into a group and says, "I know you have had five youth pastors in the past four years. But I want you to know that I am here to stay. I am going to be here with you guys, no matter what. I am here to plant my heart with you, and you can trust me." Six months later, he receives a job offer from someone who is actually going to . . . pay with money! So, at the next meeting, the kids hear, "I feel the Lord leading me over here to this other job."

See what he's doing? He may claim, "I never told them I was going to be there for two years!" But didn't he imply it? He put it out there because he wanted them to trust him. Later, he walked away saying, "Well, I can't help it. God led me. I guess I was supposed to be over there the whole time."

This is not honorable. Worse, will these kids want to trust another leader in their lives?

Sadly, we all have the tendency to woo people into following us. Then we stomp on their hearts, and it's "out of sight, out of mind."

So when striving to live honorably, always ask, do I demand more from others than I'm willing to do myself? Am I just taking the easy road this time because the right

Do I demand more from others than I'm willing to do myself?

road is harder? Remember, the easy road is always . . . easier; but it often leaves honor behind.

> **Question:** *Am I living with any gray areas in my life?*

. . . must have a strong family life. It's easy to get so wrapped up in ministry that our families are lost amid our hectic activity, and their spiritual growth gets shifted to a back burner. When we realize this, we are jolted into focusing on them for a while; but before you know it, we're sucked back into the ministry again. And again and again.

Paul was very clear about the priority of families when he instructed young Timothy:

> *Now the overseer must . . . manage his own family well and see that his children obey him with proper respect. (If anyone does not know how to manage his own family, how can he take care of God's church?)*
>
> —1 Timothy 3:2, 4–5

In attempting to "manage" my own family, I've found it helps to ask myself frequently: Do I know where my kids are right now . . . spiritually?

Recently the Luce household took an eagerly anticipated vacation in Florida. We decided to begin our first day the same as we start every other day: with our quiet times.

Cameron—five years old and the proud owner of Buzz

Lightyear and Woody toys—was up early that day, looking at the pictures in his Bible. "Cameron," I asked, "did you help Woody and Buzz have their quiet times this morning?"

"No, they didn't want to have one," he answered, already feeling the pull of the Magic Kingdom.

"Maybe they need to give their hearts to the Lord, huh? Here they are, sitting right here. Want to see if they'd like to give their hearts to Jesus?"

So Cameron started into his little "altar call," saying, "Do you want to give your heart to the Lord?"—and boom, Woody's hand went up, and Buzz's hand went up too.

"Tell them what to do," I said.

"Okay, c'mon down here and kneel, Buzz and Woody."

So I helped walk the toys down to the "front," and set them on their knees.

"Can you lead them in a prayer, Cameron?"

He led them right through a prayer, and they gave their colorful, plastic lives to the Lord. And from that day on, I noticed that Cameron and his two converts often had their quiet times together, with him telling the action heroes his favorite Bible stories.

Here's the thing: I felt that I'd touched base with Cameron on a spiritual level—on his level—about our life with God. It wasn't formal and it didn't take a lot of time, but we connected. Remember: we may live in the same house with our families, eat the same food, look out the

We may live in the same house with our families, eat the same food, look out the same windows, and drive in the same car—but do we know their hearts?

same windows, and drive in the same car—but do we know their hearts?

Question: *Do I know where my children are spiritually?*

. . . must make good use of time. Wouldn't you agree that time management is a huge issue for people in youth ministry? Most of us feel stretched to the breaking point by the sheer number of things—good things—we have to do in a day. But think about it: the president of General Motors has 24 hours in a day just as you do, and he manages thousands and thousands of employees. The problem is not that we don't have enough time; it's how we use the time we have.

For example, do you "leverage" your time? That is, do you choose to do only the things that will have the greatest impact (though there are many other things you could do)? It may not sound very spiritual on the surface, but Youth Specialists must get the "biggest bang for the buck" with their time.

These first four "Must Haves" relate to the heart and life of a Youth Specialist. Now let's look at six which deal

Let God begin to spark your heart with His dream!

with leadership qualities which will propel your ministry forward.

Question: *How effectively am I using my hours today?*

. . . must carry oneself with dignity. Many times the way we carry ourselves gives people a false idea of who we are. If we dress like a teenager, talk like a teenager, and swagger like, well, a teenager, others will continue to see us as "just the youth guy." Instead of getting rid of this negative stigma, we've now perpetuated it. Ask, "How do I carry myself?" The answer will reveal your true identity as a leader.

The things we do, the things we say, certain habits that show through—any of these things can give us dignity and draw people toward us . . . or cause disrespect and push people away. If you find yourself constantly wondering, *why don't these parents just support me?* check your Dignity Quotient. If you're acting like a kid, they'll treat you like a kid. Or if you feel like a second-class citizen, they'll treat you like . . . you get the picture, right?

How you carry yourself will determine how much credibility you have. You may think, "But I'm in youth ministry, I don't care what adults think of me." You should care. You need the older body of Christ to stand with you in reaching the younger generation. The great thing is that if they believe in you, then they'll believe in your vision. If they believe in your vision, they'll fund your vision.

It's all about credibility. Others won't believe in your plan—no matter how great—if they don't believe in you.

Question: *What aura do I radiate as a person and a leader?*

. . . *must dream big.* God wants to give you a dream. Why? Because if you can't dream it, it won't happen. God honored Joseph because he dared to dream. In the same way, God is excited to hear you say, "Wow, look at this amazing thing—it's grown! It's doubled every year for the last three years! Just like I imagined." He wants you to tune out the noise long enough to hear His voice and dream His dream.

A lot of people live empty lives, even in the ministry, because they refuse to dream. They go to this meeting and that meeting, and they wear themselves out. They care about kids, but they are not fulfilled. There's something about dreaming that fuels your fire and ignites fulfillment.

There are no limitations to dreaming. You might think, "I'm just a youth pastor at this church. How does this apply

Others won't believe in your plan
—no matter how great—if they
don't believe in you.

to me?" I'm simply saying that the size of your church should have absolutely nothing to do with the size of your youth ministry. According to the national average, 10 percent of the church is youth. If you have less than 10 percent, you don't even have all the kids who come to your church! If you are doing more than that, you are beating the odds.

I think all of us should beat the odds. Why? Because it is up to us to populate the next generation for Christianity. Sadly, some big churches have four or five thousand members but only about two hundred kids in the youth group. They don't even have all the kids who come to the church.

As you can tell, I am less impressed with numbers than ratios here. God's perspective requires dreaming big to outpace the averages. If you have 100 people in your church and 10 kids in your youth group, that's great. But don't stop there! You could have 100 kids—or more! In fact, I know of churches that have to swap room assignments on Wednesday nights. The adults meet in the youth room so the overwhelming numbers of teens can use the main sanctuary for a youth service.

Could you dream something like that? Let God begin to spark your heart with His dream!

Question: *If Jesus Christ came back and was the youth pastor at my church for a year, what would it look like?*

. . . must be a planner. I admit it. I was intimidated for a long time by this whole idea of planning. It seemed

There's something about dreaming that fuels your fire and ignites fulfillment.

tedious and boring. I used to tell my staff, "God wants us to do this and this and this . . . Now go make it happen, and God bless you as you do it." Their favorite line was, "Ron dreams, and we sweat." I didn't want to plan everything out and think about money and people and programs; that stuff bored me.

Think about this for a moment: our God is a planner. Here's what He told Jeremiah about the time before there even was a Jeremiah: "Before I formed you in the womb I knew you, before you were born I set you apart; I appointed you as a prophet to the nations" (Jer. 1:5).

Now that's planning ahead!

On the other hand, I hear some youth pastors say, "I don't want to put God in a box. I want to be free, to move with the Spirit." Those are good Christian sentiments, but they can be used to cover a subtle form of laziness. Isn't it true that sometimes we just don't want to pay the price in terms of desk time and sweating through the details? Or maybe we don't know how.

It's true I haven't always been a planner, and for a long time I just wanted to stick with "preach and pray." In fact, I

It is critical to recognize that we must first widen our cups to catch more of the fruit we are harvesting.

did everything in the world to avoid planning. You could always find me mowing the lawn, doing stuff around the facilities, or fiddling with projects around my house.

Why? Because dreaming is one thing; planning to make that dream a reality is another. Be encouraged. One of the most exciting eras of my ministry kicked in after I learned how to plan.

Question: *Can I discipline myself to slow down and think through the whole process—regularly?*

. . . must be a builder. The apostle Paul was a builder —one who devised a plan and strategically pursued it with a final, lasting structure in mind. At first glance, his journeys to visit the early churches might appear to be random ministry, with six months here, nine months there, and a year and a half somewhere else—a sort of early house-to-house visitation. Not so! Look again at how he revisited those converts for follow-up and never failed to write them letters—even from prison! Paul was conscious of building something significant.

Remember the parable of the sower? How many times have we haphazardly "spread our seeds" without thinking about where they would land? But if you could choose to use your energy to plant seeds that went only into good ground, why would you also drop them onto rocks? Few people use their energy strategically.

The momentum that drives a youth ministry forward is nothing other than a firm conviction of God's call and bold faith.

What does it mean if a youth guy says: "Yes, I was at First Church, but then I felt led by the Lord to go over to Second Church"?

I'll tell you what it means to me: this person probably wasn't in the middle of building something at First Church! When you are invested in building a house, you don't just walk away from it. Neither would you casually leave a youth ministry made effective by the certainty that you are laboring together with God to build something significant, something eternal.

Unless you like walking around in circles.

Unless you like the ministry merry-go-round.

Wouldn't you rather stay and build something that will last and become a legacy?

Question: *How am I using my personal energy?*

. . . must grow as a leader. If you find that you and your ministry helpers are simply "doing what you've always

done," then you are probably leading by default. It's easy to slide into this pattern even with the best of intentions. But if you'll learn how to lead with purpose, the results in changed lives will be multiplied. Sure, the status quo is always much more comfortable than taking up the task of figuring out how to most effectively transform the present situation for the kingdom. When you learn how to be the leader God wants you to be, your dreams will become a reality, and your job will be a lot more fun.

Consider what I call the leadership cup theory. (I'll explain this more fully in Chapter 3.) Every one of you has a leadership cup that can hold a certain number of youth. Your youth group can grow only as large as the capacity of your cup. We all get frustrated in ministry when we try to grow our group without growing our leadership cup. It is critical to recognize that we must first widen our cups to catch more of the fruit we are harvesting. Thus, growing as a leader means widening your cup.

I once asked Dr. Bill Bright, founder of Campus Crusade, what he had done to develop himself as a leader over the years. He said, "I'm just a voracious reader." He reads constantly—the Bible, of course, but also every form of leadership material he can get his hands on. He is a great example to follow.

Question: *Am I leading only by default these days?*

Your firm recognition of a heavenly calling doesn't mean it will always be easy.

... must have formidable faith. What does it mean for you to have a deep faith in God? I can only tell you how it plays out in my life. Nineteen years ago when Katie and I started Teen Mania Ministries, we sent out support letters to everyone we knew—just 120 people. Every day, we'd run to the mailbox to see whether anyone had sent us some support money. After about three weeks, we had a grand total of three checks. That was all the money ever to come from those 120 letters.

"Katie," I said, "we've got to do this ministry. I don't know if people understand what we are doing, but we have to do it anyway." So we took the first shaky step of faith.

I remember being on the road, calling any place in the world just to get the name of a church. If I had a friend in a particular city, I'd ask him, "Could you mail me a phone book from your town?" Then I'd look in the Yellow Pages for churches in the area.

I finally pulled together a little itinerary and we left home in October for six weeks on the road. We traveled all through the South and held rallies at night with massive crowds of 10 and 20 people at a time.

We packed out living rooms all across America!

We would do about two or three meetings a week, take offerings, and live on whatever was graciously placed into "the hat." (Do you know what it's like to live off teenage offerings? That takes some faith.)

In those early days there were countless last-minute cancellations. We didn't have an office yet and packed everything in our little car. We'd arrive two or three days before a service with all our gear in tow and stay in a host home until it was time to leave for the next church. So when someone called to cancel, that would mean no place for Ron and Katie to stay for a couple of days. Since we seldom had more than $200 in the bank at any given time, shelling out money for lodging or unexpected car repairs was a continual opportunity to practice our faith!

I can just hear the violins playing in the background, but let me say from experience: faith sustains us through everything. Katie and I knew one thing: God called us to a task, and we had to do it. It didn't matter if no one believed in us, everything worked against us, and we had no money—because our calling was so real. It was from God and depended upon God. We had to act in faithful obedience.

It takes boldness and faith like that to be a Youth Specialist. Without it, you can pack up, go home, and pull out the classifieds. There are easier ways to make a living, but is there a more fulfilling, rewarding life?

Your firm recognition of a heavenly calling doesn't mean it will always be easy. I know people walk into *Acquire the Fire* events each week, see auditoriums filled with five to ten thousand teens, and think, *Oh, look at all these kids. It must have been easy for him.* No, it wasn't. But we had a clear mission and an unshakable belief that God would accomplish

Question: *Do I have the boldness to go for it?*

His purposes. The momentum that drives a youth ministry forward is nothing other than a firm conviction of God's call and bold faith.

After all, God never called us to do something that was *possible*. If we think it's *possible*, we're not dreaming big enough.

CHAPTER THREE

Beginning the Leadership Journey

Leadership. It's very much a buzzword today. But what exactly is leadership, and how does it actually affect my youth ministry? The title above should give you a hint—that's what this chapter is about. Understanding godly leadership will be the framework for the rest of this book.

There's a big difference between growing as a leader and growing as a minister; there's also a big difference between growing as a leader and growing as a Christian. I always thought that the closer I got to Jesus, the better leader I would be. But the two don't necessarily go together. Just because you grow as a Christian doesn't necessarily mean you become a better leader. Just as you

Just as you need to be deliberate about growing in your relationship with Jesus Christ, you also need to be deliberate about developing your leadership skills.

need to be deliberate about growing in your relationship with Jesus Christ, you also need to be deliberate about developing your leadership skills.

Your passion for God and continual growth as a Christian is the foundation of godly leadership. Let your heart for the Lord grow and your love for Him explode! Never back down on meditating on the Word and letting Him increase your spiritual fire. This vibrant spiritual health is the cornerstone on which you build a model of Christlike leadership. Effective leadership requires us to exercise and develop *both* our relationship with God and our skills as a leader.

What does it look like if you are a well-developed minister and Christian, but not a developed leader?

Maybe you've seen a church or a ministry where the preacher is just incredible. I mean, fire from heaven is spilling from his lips and it just rips at your soul. His preaching gets you fired up, but you wonder why there are only 50 people to hear him? *This is so good there ought to be thousands here!* You scratch your head and wonder why it's such a small group. Perhaps it's because that preacher is very developed as a minister, but not very developed as a leader. Other times, you may see the ministry of a big church with lots of programs, small groups, and even a television ministry. But their preacher is nowhere near the same level as the other preacher you heard. That person is very developed as a leader but not as a minister. You don't have to choose between one and the other. There are many ministers who have developed as both a minister and a leader.

It is essential for a Youth Specialist to develop both dimensions. When you have a small youth group, the pastor says, "You need to be faithful with the few." But if, after 20 years of ministry there are still only 10 or 20 youth, and the ministry is not growing or flourishing as it should be—it's time to take a closer look. It all rests on leadership development. If you don't grow as a leader, your group will not grow either.

On the other hand, you may hold an outreach event, get a ton of kids there, and see 50 of them get saved! But two weeks later you'll still have the same 10 kids you started out with, even after you had this incredible outreach. How could that happen? It's not that you need more activities. What you need to do is learn how to catch a lot of fish and *keep them* once they've been caught.

When you grow as a leader you begin to discover how to keep them in the boat. Part of that hinges on understanding the leadership cup theory. It goes like this:

Each one of us has a cup—our leadership cup. One person's cup is 10 people big; another's is 20 people big. Some might hold 50 or 100. Whatever the size your cup is, that is the number of people your leadership skills have equipped you to lead. You can do every outreach and evangelism project you can think of, but if you have a 10-person cup, that will be the limit of your group. That's all you're capable of leading. Your group will never grow.

If you don't grow as a leader, your group will not grow either.

You could try another outreach, do more activities—work yourself to death—but your group would still be limited to the same number of people that fit in your cup. However big your cup, that's how big your group stays. The extra ones won't fit in there and will just spill over the top.

This is where some "youth guys" will quit. They start believing that God only wants 10 in their group, since no matter what they do the group doesn't increase. We need to be careful here—don't let your experience dictate your theology. Maybe you don't have more youth because you haven't grown your leadership cup before you tried to grow your group.

The good news is that you can expand your cup. That's what growing as a leader is all about: learning how to expand your leadership cup. This is what will catch the fish and keep them in the boat.

Maybe you still don't see a reason why you should grow as a leader. I understand. For a long time, I felt the same way.

10 REASONS WHY I NEVER GREW AS A LEADER

1. I didn't know that I should be growing as a leader. I thought just growing as a Christian was enough. It's like being lost. If you're lost, and you know it, then you can look at a map and get direction. But if you're lost, and you don't know it, then you'll just keep doing the same things and never think of trying to find a way out.

I didn't know that I should be growing as a leader. I thought I was fine, since I was on fire for God. What else did I need? I thought leadership training was only for people that were going to be the presidents of corporations or nations. Presidents need to learn about leadership, but ministers, like myself, need to learn about ministry.

That was just ignorant and no one ever told me anything different. Well, now I'm telling you. You can and must grow as a leader.

2. *I didn't know how to grow.* It's easy to say that you should grow as a leader. But how? Where do you start? Wouldn't it be great if there were just a leadership pill? You could just take the pill—bam! You are now a robust leader. I haven't found that yet. If you find it, please let me know.

I'd love to take that pill. In the meantime, I'll give you tips on how to grow as a leader. Continue to educate yourself. There are plenty of other resources out there that focus exclusively on leadership; I'll be focusing more on how it applies to being a Youth Specialist.

3. *I didn't know where to start.* Once I realized how lost I was and how ignorant I was, I got really frustrated. When we first started the ministry, my leadership was more like a bull in a china shop. My leadership "horns" were knocking everything over, breaking things, but I didn't notice because I was "so on fire for God."

I was running over my staff and making their lives miserable. I was dreaming big and all my staff were just getting worn out. "More vision" to them only meant that they had to pedal faster. I had no idea where to begin to fix things. Finally, I realized I needed to change myself.

But where to begin? The list of all the things I was doing wrong as a leader was so long, I didn't even know where to start. It's pretty embarrassing, but it's true.

If you don't grow as a leader, you won't influence a many people.

4. I couldn't find any leadership direction in the Bible. I'd been reading through the Bible, and I couldn't find any chapter where it said, "A good leader does _____." I would read and read, and ask, "Where's the leadership chapter?"

Of course, 1 Timothy talks about the qualifications of a leader—his life and character—but it doesn't give the "10 Action Steps to Be a Wise Leader." I discovered if you're not used to looking for leadership principles, you won't see them in the Word.

I had to start somewhere, so I started reading leadership books, listening to tapes, and going to seminars where they laid leadership principles out for me. Then, like a bloodhound, I caught the scent of leadership. I knew what it smelled like, and suddenly I could see it all through the Bible. Now I can look through the Word and leadership principles leap out at me. Once I was trained to recognize what to look for I could see it; before that I was blind to it.

5. I didn't think it really mattered. I thought as long as I was passionate about the vision, passionate about God, that was all I needed. Yes, that was sufficient for my own personal relationship with Him. But what about sharing His grace with others?

If you don't grow as a leader, you won't influence many people. You'll have great times alone with God, but you'll be alone in your ministry, because people don't want to come to watch you and God be alone.

You can only run on passion for so long. Running on passion burns other people out. When you're passionate, you drive yourself hard and you drive others hard too. When my people burned out, I dismissed it. "They just weren't committed enough." I was wrong. I finally realized I had to develop something besides passion.

6. I thought leaders were born, not made. Have you ever felt that way? You see people who make awe-inspiring leadership decisions, and you think, "Man, how do they do that?"

These people used to make me mad. I remember growing up jealous of the "natural leaders" at my schools. I figured they were born with their ability, and because I didn't have any, I gave up. Some of you may think, "I just don't have the gift." This is not true. As you look around, people may look like they're born leaders, but there are often other circumstances you don't see. Perhaps there were other leaders in the family who modeled those skills for them—an older brother, for example, who was the captain of the ball team. Maybe there were parents who coached or ran a store and exhibited leadership traits.

No matter what your age, you can surround yourself with good quality leadership material, whether it's reading, listening to tapes, or finding mentor leaders in your life. Surround yourself with those influences because it's never too late to acquire leadership skills.

I was not a natural leader—in fact the only thing I was good at naturally was being obnoxious (and I was really good at that). As a result, I was the last person you would ever want to follow. I've had to work hard to develop leadership ability.

7. I couldn't see how growing as a leader applied to ministry. I always thought leadership applied to business, politics, and government, but how does it apply to ministry? I thought if someone gave a great altar call, that made him a great leader (I was wrong—that makes him a

You can only run on passion for so long. Running on passion burns other people out.

After the altar call is when evangelism ends and leadership begins.

great evangelist). After the altar call is when evangelism ends and leadership begins.

The lack of leadership training is a huge problem in the church today. I went to college, studied the Bible, and learned about ministry, but I never learned a single thing about leadership. I never learned about management or delegation or finances. Part of every ministry—no matter how small—is its leadership/business side.

That's right, there's a business side to ministry. If you develop only the spiritual side and ignore the business/leadership side, you just won't grow. Most of the churches in the United States are for sale. Do you know why? They're run by people who hold master's degrees— sometimes PhD's—in theology, but who don't know anything about leadership. They were never trained in management or finances and drifted into the red financially. No amount of pleading for more offerings or loans of money can pay for the building and the church goes up for auction.

Church splits are another result of poor leadership. Church splits occur when weak leadership at the top doesn't keep people focused on the vision and moving in that direction. Some churches will never split because there is strong, sound biblical leadership in place. I can go into a church anywhere and tell just by the flavor and the style of leadership whether or not that church is in danger of a split.

8. I didn't realize that by not choosing a leadership style I was choosing. What do I mean by that? When I first started learning a little bit about leadership, I saw that there were different models and styles. No single style grabbed me. I thought, "I don't really want to be completely like that, and I don't really want to be like that. I won't be a pigeonholed leader. I'm just going to keep learning and stay neutral."

I didn't realize that by not choosing I was really abdicating my role. My style of leadership was haphazard. No one really knew what he could expect from me: sometimes one thing would happen, sometimes another. I was unpredictable. Unpredictable leadership destroys confidence. People wonder if they'll have a job next week; they don't know what behavior you expect from them.

Eventually, I realized that when I refused to choose a style of leadership it cost me staff. I figured out that choosing a style and committing to it was better than not choosing anything. Even a bad philosophy of leadership is better than no philosophy of leadership.

At least if you choose a philosophy, you have something to work with. If you realize part of it is bad, then you can tweak that part. But if you just fly by the seat of your pants, you don't really know what to adjust. You are swayed by whatever comes your way.

RUNNING ON PASSION

Before, we were running on pure passion, but after using the [principles in this book], I was amazed at . . . how our youth ministry became well-rounded, and we grew spiritually, not just numerically. I found out you can't run a youth ministry based on passion alone.

—Brandon, Youth Specialist

If God has called you to lead a ministry,
youth ministry, youth group, church,
then He has made you smart
enough to lead it!

9. I didn't think I was smart enough. I'll be honest with you; I didn't think I was smart enough to be a world-class leader. I saw really smart people leading awesome ministries, and I thought, "Who am I?" I knew I was smart enough to love God. I was smart enough to stay close to God, have good quiet times, and give a good sermon every now and then. But I didn't think I was really smart enough to be a leader. There was so much to learn and do, and I was just . . . well, me. I lacked confidence.

The breakthrough for me came when I gave my life to Christ and learned that my value and worth are found in Him. Here's what I learned: people are just people. Any of us can develop our potential to learn and grow. Geniuses aren't the only ones allowed to be great leaders; the rest of us can be too.

If God has called you to lead a ministry, youth ministry, youth group, church, then He has made you smart enough to lead it!

10. I didn't understand that ministry, leadership, and management all work together. I thought I could just pray and preach and let other people build the organization. But ministry, leadership, and management all work together. You can have a great ministry vision, but if you can't lead people, you'll be working alone; and if you can't manage the ministry, it will fall apart.

The most successful ministries integrate all three things. If you're lacking one of them, you're trying to operate a tripod ministry on only two legs. A dream won't motivate people by itself; they have to see leadership that's dedicated to accomplishing it. As coach Tom Landry said, "Leadership is getting someone to do what they don't want to do, to achieve what they want to achieve." People want to achieve ministry, but it takes a leader to get them there.

WHY SHOULD YOU GROW AS A LEADER?

So you won't rob people of their chance to hear the Gospel. Up to this point, you may still believe that growth as a leader is an option. Listen carefully: If you don't grow as a leader, you may rob people of their chance to be saved. Youth who could be affected by your ministry won't be. Kids who could grow in the Lord won't grow.

What if honing your leadership skills means that your youth group will grow from its current 10 or 20 or 30 kids, to 300 in a year . . . wouldn't it be worth it? Think, too, about all those kids who wouldn't be in your group a year from now if you didn't grow as a leader—you'd be robbing them of their chance to be impacted by the Word of God through you. When you grow as a leader, you grow your leadership cup, and the number of people you can minister to grows. It's not an exact science. You just start to think differently: deliberately and strategically. Your ability to lead grows.

So you can treat those who work with you respectfully. When you have vision and passion for your youth ministry,

If you don't grow as a leader, you may rob people of their chance to be saved. Youth who could be affected by your ministry won't be.

When you don't grow as a leader, you run over people in the name of passion for the Lord.

but don't grow as a leader, you disrespect the people who have volunteered to help you.

I used to think that the only people who were really committed were the ones on my staff who worked hours of overtime like I did. I believed they were the best workers. I was glad they were as committed as I was . . . until their wives began to complain that they never saw their husbands and their kids wondered where their daddy was. Even then, I didn't think it was a serious problem—after all, they were impacting youth for God's kingdom.

I started to dream bigger, and told them I needed more effort even though they were working 20 hours a day. I wasn't a good enough leader to recognize that they needed balance in their lives.

When you don't grow as a leader, you run over people in the name of passion for the Lord. All you care about is the vision. Your ministry may be growing, but your people aren't. Leadership means taking care of your staff and your youth so that they can take care of the vision.

So you can better serve those you lead. We do our teens a disservice by not growing as leaders because we can't serve them as well. In the early days, I thought that the leader was the guy who told everybody else what to do. Once you become a leader you find out the leader is the one who serves others.

Many of you have discovered that being a leader is a lot more work than what you first thought it was. It's not just holding the microphone.

You need to learn best how to serve your teens. How can you help them have better quiet times? How can you help them grow? How can they have a better worship time? If you don't develop yourself as a leader, you won't serve them well.

Before I started to grow as a leader, I read motivational books about leadership, but I didn't take them seriously. I thought, "It's not like there's a test on this material." But *there* is a test on it. The test is life. The test is every Wednesday and every Sunday. The test is meeting with your leaders. The test is how you carry yourself. Life is your test, and if you fail, you've just failed all the kids in your group and all the kids who could have been in your group.

You need to decide right now. Are you committed to growing as a leader, so that you can better evangelize and equip your teens?

HOW DO YOU ACTUALLY GROW AS A LEADER?

Transform your mind. This is what I do. I take four or five main points from a book, type them out, put them in bullet points on a piece of paper, and carry it around with me. Then I use it in my quiet time and pray those leadership principles into my life. The Bible tells us in Romans 12:2 that we are transformed by the renewing of our minds. So I would renew my mind with leadership principles. Since I

> Many of you have discovered that being a leader is a lot more work than what you first thought it was. It's not just holding the microphone.

You must train yourself to think like a leader, like a wise general. We are in a battle for the souls of a whole generation.

was *not* a natural leader, I had to train my mind to go in that direction.

I had to learn how to think, talk, and act as a leader. I would drill in those four or five points, and then I'd read another book and add four or five more points. Read another book, add four or five more points. Pretty soon I'd internalized a lot of information. Part of my quiet time was spent praying; part was in the Word; but I also always meditated over leadership principles because I wanted to grow as a leader.

I encourage you to do this as you begin your quest to become a better leader. I listen to tapes all the time and take notes—you can too. Once you start to recognize leadership principles, you'll be able to listen to preaching tapes that aren't necessarily about leadership, and "sniff them out" there, too.

Eventually I got to the point where I could listen to a pastor telling an anecdote and tell what style of leadership he uses by the way he interacts with his staff in the story. It's really not the point of his sermon, but I can understand how he acts as a leader. You too can recognize leadership principles everywhere.

Ask questions. Don't be afraid to ask questions. I ask questions wherever I go. If I'm at a rental car counter, for example, and I see an employee who has a badge that says "12 years of service," then I stop and talk to her. I'll ask, "What has made you want to stay here for 12 years?" What

I want to learn is who led her to a place where she would commit 12 years of her life to rent cars to people. I would like workers who are that loyal. So what does a rental car company do that I'm not doing? I'm willing to learn from Avis. I might ask a pastor, "What do you do for your staff meetings? What makes people want to be here?" You can learn from anybody.

You must train yourself to think like a leader, like a wise general. We are in a battle for the souls of a whole generation. We'd better begin to think like generals and leaders. Yes, we need to grow as Christians and ministers, but we can't stop there. We must grow as leaders in order to reach this generation.

As you begin to do these things and meditate on the leadership principles, you'll find your leadership cup will grow a little bit without your realizing it. Pretty soon you'll be thinking differently, managing differently, and there'll be 20 kids in your group. And it will grow from there.

Wouldn't it be great if there were hundreds of ministries in your region with a hundred or more kids in each youth group? Wouldn't it be fantastic to see youth ministries all over the place with a thousand kids coming every week? Shouldn't there be? Doesn't it make you mad that the devil's youth group is bigger than ours? The world knows how to organize and lead and plan, and so must we if we want to influence a lot of people.

We all know youth ministry is hard work. So if we are going to work hard, we might as well do the right work— the work of a leader—so we can have maximum impact on lives.

The rest of this book will give you practical tools to develop your youth ministry and yourself as a leader. You will learn the imperative, behind-the-scenes work of a leader. You will learn time-tested principles that work for our ministry and for thousands of youth ministries around the country. But it *is* work. Be ready to read and work in each chapter.

The good news is that the frustration of not knowing what to do is about to end. You will have a very clear picture of what to do. We all know youth ministry is hard work. So if we are going to work hard, we might as well do the right work—the work of a leader—so we can have maximum impact on lives.

Take some time and ask God to open up your heart to the leadership potential He has for you.

Then keep reading.

CHAPTER FOUR

I Have a Dream

Martin Luther King was not the only one to proclaim this statement with great boldness. These are the words of every great leader.

Moses had a dream of going to the promised land. Abraham had a dream of going into another land. Joseph dreamed about being a great leader. This is God's model of leadership in the Bible. He chooses a person, gives him or

Every great work for the Lord starts with a dream.

her a dream, and gathers others around to help accomplish that dream together.

Every great work for the Lord starts with a dream. Every great leader has a dream, a glimpse down the path of spiritual transformation where you will lead others. You may not have contacts, money, helpers, or facilities, but if you have a dream you have the most important ingredient!

When I speak of a dream I am talking about vision— opening your eyes to see what God sees, and to feel His heartbeat for teens in your town.

> *Where there is no revelation [or prophetic vision], the people cast off restraint.*
> —Proverbs 29:18 (NKJV)

In these few words is a powerful truth. Without a vision or dream, people have no restraint, no way to harness their energy for productive use. Vision is the bridle that couples energy with purpose, and generates the power of horses pulling a huge stagecoach! Today, we have a generation without a vision—they use their energy for this and that, with no direction or restraint. The end result? We have a lot of kids in church who are fooling around, getting into trouble, and living compromised Christian lives because there is nothing harnessing their energy to use for God.

Whether or not to have big dreams isn't an option. It is mandatory! A sports coach recognizes this and sets a vision for his team: "This is where we are going to go; this is what we can become!" His vision inspires them to run and sweat and work hard. It focuses their passion and energy.

Sadly, our youth groups suffer because we don't dare to dream. We wonder why our students haven't gotten fired up, done something for God, risen up to take their school back—much less take America back. Yet, we are the ones who must paint the picture for them. We have to dream it first and show them where they fit into our vision. Don't expect them to figure it out themselves. We must compel them with our vision to go for it!

When we talk about dreams and visions, let's dream big. If we are going to see something huge happen here in North America for the cause of Christ for young people, it has to be about more than just filling arenas and stadiums. Don't get me wrong; God has a use for arenas and stadiums. I'm just glad that someone else built them for us! (They think that they built them for basketball teams and football teams and rock concerts. But they really built them for the kingdom of God.) The fact is, if God is the foundation of our dreams, we won't be limited to just filled arenas and stadiums. We ought to see youth ministries that go from 10 to 50 and then from 50 to 100 and then from 100 to 200 and then from 200 to 500 and then 500 to 1,000. All over America, there ought to be thousands and thousands of youth ministries that have a thousand or two thousand or three thousand teens.

Some time ago, I heard about a youth group down in Bogotá, Colombia, that draws 40,000 teens every week. Forty thousand! I had to see it for myself. When I walked into the arena, I saw 20,000 teens—and they fill it twice each Saturday! Each week, 2,500 teens give their lives to Jesus, and all the youth are involved in 13,000 cell groups. See what can happen with a vision!

So, yes, I am all for dreaming big. I just don't think you can outdream God. He "is able to do exceedingly abundantly above all that we ask or think" (Eph. 3:20 NKJV). If we can think it, He can do far more. So we are the only ones limiting God when we think tiny or dream small.

I just don't think you can outdream God.

When you dream big, you must consider not just the size, but the nature of the group. Will they be soul winners, passionate for God? Will they be hungry Christians? What does it matter if you have the biggest group in the city if they're all lukewarm? Mere size is not the issue; size is only important because it means that you are reaching more people. You must still make sure that you are really reaching them. Part of your vision has to include how you are reaching them and how you are truly discipling them. Are they really growing strong? Are they in the Word? Dreaming big is the key.

LET'S TALK ABOUT WHY WE DON'T DREAM

"Having a small group keeps me humble." *"Well, God wants to keep me humble, and I just want to be a humble servant of the Lord."* This one really grates on me. I have heard leaders excuse themselves: "If God has called you to be the youth pastor of 10 kids your entire life, then you ought to be content with that." What? God is a God of destiny! He is a God of potential! Where you are now is never where He wants you to remain. "Potential" means those things that you haven't done yet. If you've already done something, it is no longer potential. Our God is a God who sees the very best and raises people up and breathes life and dreams into them. Besides, small does not necessarily mean humble. You can be small in size, but still haughty and arrogant in your attitude.

"Having a small group keeps my pride in check." *"I might get prideful if my group gets big, so God is keeping it small."* This is simply another twist on the last point. So instead of dealing with your own sin issues, you will just let the kids you haven't yet reached go to hell? No, this is just an excuse to keep from following God's bigger plan: God's plan is always for us to share His Good News with more people.

"I don't think I can do it." "I can't do it anyway, so why dream it?" This is an unholy inferiority complex. It's another twist on the first two excuses because it is, ultimately, a form of pride. "I'm too proud to trust the Almighty with my inability." The truth is, we don't have to do anything. But through God, we can change the world. If your dream is only as big as your own capacity, then it is not big enough. There isn't room for God in small dreams.

"I've failed in the past." "I've dreamed big and fallen flat on my face. How long can I keep doing that?" Most of us have tried things that failed. We've been mocked or ridiculed for past screw-ups. If you've given up on dreams, or given up on trying to do something great, or given up on functioning outside of your comfort zone or box—it is time to dream again. Some of you are still letting people beat you up for what you did two or three years ago, and it is hand-cuffing you from fulfilling your potential. Shake them off. Joseph—the Bible's best dreamer—had to fall flat several times before his big dreams were realized.

"People might scoff at my dreams." "When I tell people my vision, they tell me to be realistic." The world—even when speaking in the voice of our pastors—can be devastating to our God-given dreams. People throw cold water on your bold imagination and audacious faith. It is time to forgive those—deacons, pastors, leaders—who have mocked your dream or put you down. Don't you dare let their past infringements on your dream harness your future potential.

I can't begin to tell you how many times I have had people laugh at me when I shared what God was calling us

There isn't room for God in small dreams.

It is okay to dream big; just be careful
when and where you share
your dreams.

to do. My own board of directors used to laugh at me. Our
first summer in ministry, we had 30 young people on the
mission field. When we came back the board asked me,
"Ron, what are your goals for the next year?"

"Next summer, I want to take 200 young people on the
mission field!"

They laughed out loud! Literally! Because we had seen
others try to get more young people on the mission field,
and the most anyone could get was 30. So they laughed,
"Come on, get real! Come back down to earth. How many
do you want?"

I said, "Two hundred. I want to take 200 kids to
Guatemala."

The next summer came around and we took 260 kids,
some to Costa Rica, some to Guatemala. After the second
year they said, "Great! What an awesome summer! What an
awesome year! Now, where do you want the ministry to be
in five years?"

I said, "You know what? When we are celebrating our
five-year anniversary, I want to be taking 1,000 kids every
year to the mission field."

They laughed out loud again, but the fifth year came
and we had 1,057 on the mission field. They quit laughing.

It is okay to dream big; just be careful when and where
you share your dreams. Don't be like Joseph—who told his
brothers before they were ready to hear it—or you may end
up in a ditch like he did. Sometimes even the people you
think you can trust the most won't be able to handle your
dreams.

When we first started Teen Mania there were some

things in my heart that I never told anybody except Katie. I never shared them because sometimes when you dream big, people think you are arrogant, just like Joseph's brothers. But there's a difference between arrogance and faith in God's big dreams. I can remember when we first got the idea for Teen Mania; we were in Indonesia getting ready to go into India. We had a heart for the unreached people groups of the world, but the Lord was speaking to us so clearly about reaching young people in America.

I said, "Forget about those American teenagers. There are many people who can reach them. What about all the Muslims and Hindus and Buddhists here? They've never even had a chance!"

The Lord spoke to my heart again: "What about the young people in America?" And something flashed into my mind, which for years I kept to myself. I saw myself speaking in front of an arena filled with thousands of teenagers. It wasn't a stadium—it was an arena, and it was suddenly there and then gone again. It wasn't like I got caught up in a heavenly vision or anything; I just saw it in my mind.

I thought, "There's no reason anyone would ever come to hear me." I had no idea what that vision was all about, because I still had a heart for the nations. But I never told anybody that I was going to be speaking in front of thousands. Some things you just shouldn't say until the time is right. Until then, cherish them between you and God.

"Dreaming big is hard work." "I don't have the time or energy to do more than I'm already doing." I know you already

Dreaming is the real work of a leader.

work very hard, for such long hours, and you just don't feel like you have any more time to do anything else. It sounds like dreaming big means even more time away from the family, right? Not necessarily. Many times the problem isn't how much work you're doing; it's that your work lacks focus and isn't harnessed to your vision. As a result, you spend a lot of energy doing a variety of activities, none of which brings about a big, bold dream.

Dreaming is the real work of a leader. People think the real work is getting up in front of crowds, speaking, and preaching, but they're wrong. Dreaming is what happens before anyone ever sees you preach to an audience. Before he ever sees a big crowd, the Youth Specialist is on his knees crying out, "God, I have to dream! I have to hear what Your dream is for me and my youth ministry."

Do you know what is the great thing about dreaming God's dream? Our distinctiveness gives us each a slightly different dream. God delights in these differences and uses them to reach very diverse groups of teens. If we will just walk in the fullness of the vision God has given us, we will awaken in this generation a new determination to live for Him.

Don't fall into the trap of comparing the size or population of your youth group with the megachurch down the road. If we are in competition, we are in competition with the enemy. Remember that the devil's youth group is bigger than all of ours combined. We need to rescue the souls in his grip, and not worry about counting the ones in other churches. The devil is selling out secular concerts; rappers are dictating morals to this generation. There is a lot of work to do, and worrying about another church's numbers doesn't accomplish anything.

I hate it when the world dreams bigger than we do. I hate it when idolatrous people pack our teens into stadiums and fill them up with garbage. If they can dream about infecting a generation with garbage for profit, can't we dream about infecting them with truth for the Lord?

What are some of the things that have held you back from having a great dream? Now is a good time to turn to your computer and open your CD-ROM to the file titled "Dreaming Big." Think about the reasons you haven't dared to dream big and record these reasons on the first page.

You can either fill this page out on the computer or print out the Dream Questions and do it by hand. Then come back to the book and read on.

SO, WHY SHOULD WE DREAM?

You dream to fulfill your potential. You were born with an ability to do incredible things. In fact, you were made in the image of God (Gen 1:27). We, of all His creation, were made to be fellow creators. When you begin to dream, you tap into the creative nature that God breathed into you, and all of a sudden you begin to really live—food tastes better, the air smells fresher, and even the kids look pretty terrific!

Too many people never tap into their creative potential; they just punch a time card and go home. These people

Remember that the devil's youth group is bigger than all of ours combined. We need to rescue the souls in his grip, and not worry about counting the ones in other churches.

miss connecting with an incredible source of power and life! The truth is, you actually become more alive when you begin to dream and utilize some of the potential you were born with. The Holy Spirit dwells in us and wants nothing more than to empower us for great things. Don't die with unexploited potential.

You honor God when you dream big. God is the biggest dreamer ever. He imagined the world, the stars, and the galaxies into being. He thought up molecules and atoms. He is infinitely creative. So when you dream big, you take after your Father. You embrace being a daughter or son of the Most High by becoming more and more like Him. Look at one example of honoring God by dreaming big:

At Gibeon the LORD *appeared to Solomon during the night in a dream, and God said, "Ask for whatever you want me to give you."*

Solomon answered, "You have shown great kindness to your servant, my father David, because he was faithful to you and righteous and upright in heart. You have continued this great kindness to him and have given him a son to sit on his throne this very day.

"Now, O LORD *my God, you have made your servant king in place of my father David. But I am only a little child and do not know how to carry out my duties. Your servant is here among the people you have chosen, a great people, too numerous to count or number. So give your servant a discerning heart to govern your people and to distinguish between right and wrong. For who is able to govern this great people of yours?"*

The LORD *was pleased that Solomon had asked for this. So God said to him, "Since you have asked for this and not for long life or wealth for yourself, nor have asked for the death of your enemies but for discernment in administering justice, I will do what you have asked. I will give you a wise and discerning heart, so that there will never have been any-one like you, nor will there ever be. Moreover, I will give you what you have not asked for—both riches and honor—so that in your lifetime you will have no equal among kings."*

—1 Kings 3:5–13

Solomon honored God by dreaming bigger than short-term, personal gain. And God responded by going above and beyond Solomon's hopes and expectations.

There are people at the other end of your dream. If we don't dream, there are people who will never be touched by the Word. We like to say, "Well, I am just being humble," but are we being humble at the expense of other people's eternity? God wants us to have an impact on those unbelievers.

When I say to the wicked, "O wicked man, you will surely die," and you do not speak out to dissuade him from his ways, that wicked man will die for his sin, and I will hold you accountable for his blood. But if you do warn the wicked man to turn from his ways and he does not do so, he will die for his sin, but you will have saved yourself.

—Ezekiel 33:8–9

God holds us accountable to witness to the people He places in our lives. Ephesians 2:10 tells us that God has planned out works for us to do. Do not let those opportunities pass you by.

You dream to make the most of your efforts. If you don't harness your work to your dream, your energy goes

God is the biggest dreamer ever.

Are we being humble at the expense of other people's eternity?

unrestrained and undirected. It requires a lot of work to be a youth pastor. A Youth Specialist focuses the energy he already expends toward the dream. You are doing so much anyway; you might as well make it count to the max.

> Moses took his seat to serve as judge for the people, and they stood around him from morning till evening. When his father-in-law saw all that Moses was doing for the people, he said, "What is this you are doing for the people? Why do you alone sit as judge, while all these people stand around you from morning till evening?"
>
> Moses answered him, "Because the people come to me to seek God's will. Whenever they have a dispute, it is brought to me, and I decide between the parties and inform them of God's decrees and laws."
>
> Moses' father-in-law replied, "What you are doing is not good. You and these people who come to you will only wear yourselves out. The work is too heavy for you; you cannot handle it alone."
>
> —Exodus 18:15–18

Moses was a godly man who was working too hard. More specifically, he was doing work that did not move his vision for the people forward. Others had to tell him to delegate so that he could focus on the parts of his ministry that advanced God's plans. A similar situation confronted the apostles. As the church grew, so did the daily ministry needs:

> So the Twelve gathered all the disciples together and

said, *"It would not be right for us to neglect the ministry of the word of God in order to wait on tables."*

—Acts 6:2

We have servant hearts, so we're tempted to do everything that needs to be done. But God calls us to use discernment and work in a way that moves ministry forward but doesn't burn us out. This means doing the work that pursues His vision, and not simply doing a ski trip because the youth group always goes on a ski trip.

Dreaming is fun, daring, exciting, and challenging. It is very easy for us to get trapped in the comfortable routines and patterns of our lives. We know how to prepare a sermon, lead a Wednesday night study, and hang out with the kids. But our competence in those things can actually keep God from showing up with His full power.

But he said to me, "My grace is sufficient for you, for my power is made perfect in weakness." Therefore I will boast all the more gladly about my weaknesses, so that Christ's power may rest on me. That is why, for Christ's sake, I delight in weaknesses, in insults, in hardships, in persecutions, in difficulties. For when I am weak, then I am strong.

—2 Corinthians 12:9–10

When we dare to dream, we push outside the boundaries of what we can do in our own strength. We challenge and push ourselves to the outer limits of our capabilities, and in doing so, we ask God to step in.

A Youth Specialist focuses the energy he already expends toward the dream.

We challenge and push ourselves to the outer limits of our capabilities, and in doing so, we ask God to step in.

Please return to the CD-ROM file titled "Dreaming Big" and begin to dream. As before, you can either fill out page 2 on the computer or print out the Dream Questions and do it by hand.

This is the first step in launching the assault and building the ministry God has for you. Remember, there are souls on the other side of your dream.

CHAPTER FIVE

The Foundation of the Dream

No one constructs a building without first deciding how tall it should be and planning for an appropriate foundation. The foundation is the support and anchor that makes the rest of the building possible. Similarly, youth ministry demands that we think deeply about what we are building so we can lay a strong foundation.

> Youth ministry demands that we think deeply about what we are building so we can lay a strong foundation.

WHAT ARE WE BUILDING?

Then Jesus came to them and said, "All authority in heaven and on earth has been given to me. Therefore go and make disciples of all nations, baptizing them in the name of the Father and of the Son and of the Holy Spirit, and teaching them to obey everything I have commanded you. And surely I am with you always, to the very end of the age."

—Matthew 28:18–20

Matthew 28:18–20 is known as the Great Commission. Many teens don't even know what it is, and judging by how well most Christians obey what Jesus said in this passage, the "Great Suggestion" might be a better term. Yet, the foundation for youth ministry can only be this: *a vision for the whole world.*

WHY THE GREAT COMMISSION AS A FOUNDATION?

It's the most important order Jesus gave us. How important is the Great Commission? Think about it. After three years of teaching and performing miracles, Jesus died and rose from the dead. These words—the last desires He expressed to His closest friends—were their final "marching orders" before He ascended to heaven. The words emphasized what He had taught them so many times before: *reaching the world.*

This has been God's heart from the very beginning, and He wants His people to have the same driving passion.

Look at Matthew 24:14. "And this gospel of the kingdom will be preached in the whole world as a testimony to all nations, and then the end will come." The end hasn't come because the job is not yet done! This must be the foundation of our dream. Our vision must be to train up a generation of young people crafted for this specific purpose and excited to get the job done. This is the kind of Christian that we want to pump out. Youth ministry has to get away from the attitude of simply begging kids to come to church, to read their Bibles, and to stay committed to God. This self-centered focus is not what Christ called us to do.

Revelation 7:9 tells us that, one day, every tribe, every tongue, every nation, and every language will gather at the throne of grace. Every group will have a representative around the throne, and then Jesus is going to return. Today there are still 10,000 different people groups without a church.[1] If God is reserving His Son's return until this happens, we'd better make sure the dream of our youth ministry is in line with His purpose.

Jesus sent His disciples out. Think about Jesus and His disciples. He sent them out for two weeks, brought them back, and talked about the world. Then He sent out 72 more for two weeks, brought them back, and talked about the world. Jesus started with a vision for Judea and Jerusalem and expanded it to the *ends of the earth*. When we confine our thinking to our own Jerusalem, our purpose becomes too small. Yes, it is good to reach our own city, but clearly God doesn't intend for us to stop there. What then is the point of reaching teens in our town? Is it just to build a big youth group? What is God's perspective on blessing a youth group and making it large? He is looking for an army with a passion to influence the people He loves and gave His life for.

It answers the "why?" question. Why get strong in the Lord? Why be discipled? Why live a holy life? Why have

The end hasn't come because the job is not yet done!

quiet times? Why go to church? Why read the Bible? Why live in purity? Why stay away from drugs and alcohol?

Of course the typical answer given is "because the Bible says so." But *why* does the Bible say to live this way? The answer lies in God's character: our God is a holy God. He calls us to live this way because He needs an army that is disciplined and prepared to represent Him well. When we represent Him well, *that's* when and how we'll reach the world!

God's heart is for people. Moses was the youth pastor of three million people. I call him a youth pastor because the people he led were all about 40 years younger than he was. His ministry started with an encounter with God. He saw the fire and the burning bush and knew he had met with God. We as leaders need to make sure that we also have a personal *encounter* with God—what else do we have to give our kids? I'm not talking about simply praying to the Lord. I am talking about baring your soul before God, getting real with Him, and worshiping Him like the angels do. We need to get personal and real with no distractions.

Moses started with just such a personal interaction. As a result, when he spoke to the kids (the children of Israel), he spoke with authority: "I talked to I AM and HE sent me with a message. I am not fooling around here and I am not doing this because I have nothing else better to do. I can't do anything else; I've been given a message."

That message is revealed in Exodus 3:7: "I have indeed seen the misery of my people." When you get close to God's heart, you will hear Him talk about His people around the world. So many times, all we think about are the people who speak English or the people we see at the ball games. While the people around us are important and need to be incorporated into our dream, we also need to see the big picture—people around the world. Most of the people in your own town have been exposed to the Gospel, but billions around the world have *never had a chance* to hear of Jesus.

Let's look at the statistics: Out of six billion people in the world, two billion are Christians; that leaves four billion left to reach. Of those four billion, about two billion *have never had a chance to hear* the Good News (about 10,000 language groups make up those two billion people.)[2]

God says, "People are in misery. I have heard them crying out because of their slave drivers." Sin is that slave driver to the people of the world who have never had a chance to hear the Word of God. We need to listen to God and hear His heart for the people of the world, realizing that whatever we do to lead these people out of Egypt (each teen has his own Egypt) we lead them out *for a purpose.*

Why did Moses persevere even when the people did not want to follow him? He knew he had a mandate from heaven. He had heard from the burning bush, and he knew God's heart for His people. God's leader must keep the vision alive and real in front of the people regardless of whether those people agree or not.

We as leaders must resolve to build a youth ministry with God's heart for the world at the center. Our focus should be: "In some way, my kids are going to impact the four billion." You may not reach all four billion, but you might reach 400 or 4,000 or a million of them over the next 10 years as you send some of your youth out on missions trips, some into full-time outreach, and some to become evangelists. The point is we must raise up a generation that cares about the world. Even if teens are not involved in full time ministry for the rest of their lives, they need to have the lost world beating so strongly in their hearts that they continually live to find a way to impact the nations.

If we don't have money or parental support, it doesn't matter. We will help parents and leaders to understand that their children are meant to be *world changers.* If you have no

The point is we must raise up a generation that cares about the world.

pastoral support, that's okay. Convince your pastor of the biblical foundation behind your dream, and you'll get it. Don't let obstacles discourage you. Let God's vision for the nations be the foundation of your big dream. There is no bigger dream than to reach the world.

WHAT DOES "HAVING AN IDENTITY" MEAN TO MY GROUP?

Missions is our DNA. A young person gains a deep sense of Christian identity when he or she makes an impact on someone who otherwise wouldn't have had a chance to hear the Gospel. All of a sudden, it becomes much bigger than *me, my* town, where *my* eyes can see, where *I* have been, where *I* have driven before.

> *The LORD had said to Abram, "Leave your country, your people and your father's household and go to the land I will show you. I will make you into a great nation and I will bless you; I will make your name great, and you will be a blessing. I will bless those who bless you, and who- ever curses you I will curse; and all peoples on earth will be blessed through you."*
> *So Abram left, as the LORD had told him.*
> —Genesis 12:1–4a

In the days of Abraham, God set a people aside because He wanted to bless "all peoples on earth." Today, God is still in the business of blessing the peoples on the earth through those who are faithful to Him. Every church and every youth group should be urged to ask: "How can we affect the whole world?" We are here for a purpose larger than ourselves and need to find our connecting point with Abraham and his purpose: "How can I be a blessing to others on this earth?"

We can never afford—as a church—to merely talk about our blessings and once in a while listen to a visiting missionary. Like Abraham, we have a mandate from God: to be a blessing to the world. What does this mean? Does it mean that everything in our whole youth ministry should revolve around missions? Well, if we see students impacting the world as the basis of our dream, then . . . yes. That perspective will color everything else that we do. We won't do anything for the sake of doing it. We will purposefully cultivate in our teens a view to bless the world.

As stated previously, we want kids to be like young David, who, as a youth, killed a bear, a lion, and a giant. He made an impact for the Lord in Saul's court and everywhere else he went. The whole world was amazed as he represented a living God. Let's train up young men and women who will have that kind of impact!

Look also at John Mark. He met Paul at his mother's

ALL OVER THE WORLD!

I started off with no experience, and the group had no sense of direction of purpose. Now, three years later, we have grown tremendously, and there is a sense of purpose . . . We have sent countless students and adults all over the world!

—Youth Specialist

Our job is to help people understand that this is not only about you or your town—it's about the world.

house after Peter escaped from prison, and was only 14 when he went on his first mission trip with Paul and Barnabas. Later, John Mark was with Paul in prison and helped him to write letters. Later still, John Mark wrote one of the four Gospels. Traveling with the "missions team" didn't get missions *out* of his system; it got missions *into* his system!

Our job is to help people understand that this is not only about you or your town—it's about the world. We must hear the call of the Great Commission as more than just a cultural metaphor in the Bible. It is the *foundation* of the Bible. The whole Bible describes God's mission heart. He is intervening in human history and He wants us to partner with Him.

Acquire the Fire and Teen Mania sponsor a lot of mission trips, but not because missions is a fun teen thing. Missions is *THE thing*. Missions—being a blessing to all nations—is the heartbeat of purpose in the church. There is a world yet to be reached, and we aim to be a part of finishing the task. Every dream with a solid foundation will have this same conviction.

We are a part of something BIG. Each of us will have a different expression of God's dream. Your dream will be different from everyone else's and that is great. We all must aim at something big. And the world is a pretty big thing to aim at.

If our purpose is smaller than *reaching the world*, then our kids will find a bigger purpose that will demand more of them. If we don't give them something huge to be a part of, then they will find it elsewhere. We will hear them say, *"My youth group is fine, but my soccer team is going to the national championship."* Or, *"My choir is going to sing before the president."* And, *"Our band will be in this year's Rose Parade."*

If you don't share God's big purpose with them—to reach the world—they will find something bigger than your youth group. They'll go to some world-famous, secular concert with 20,000 other kids and feel like they are a part of something momentous. As a result they will find their identity in the counterfeit things of the world rather than in the authentic things of God.

We need to help them develop a mentality that says, *"We are all about rocking the world! We might be from a small town or a small youth group, but we are going to have an impact on this world."*

When we set a vision like this for our local youth ministries, our kids can be part of something significant when they become a part of our youth ministry. A vision this big requires their all, and *teens are willing to give it.* People think that youth are self-centered and lazy, but that's only because they don't have a vision to rally behind. Teens will spend hours a day working hard for a sports team or drama practice. They'll do the same if the church gives them something important to work for. But if you ask for their all, and don't have a vision that is worthy of their efforts, then you'll find yourself begging them to come back. They may come back, but their identity will be somewhere else. You will get commitment from your teens by giving them a vision that demands their all.

You know how desperately kids want to belong to something? When we ask them, "Why didn't you come to youth group?" the most common answer is, "I had practice (or some other group activity)." If that's where they've found their group identity, we'll be left like a cowboy with

As a result they will find their identity in the counterfeit things of the world rather than in the authentic things of God.

a whip trying to round up the cattle (by asking them to come back with bribes or guilt trips). On the other hand, a shepherd simply walks out in front and the sheep follow. We have to be like shepherds and give them such a great vision—a great opportunity—that they beg to come! They'll

want to know what else they can do to be involved. They'll find their identity . . . something worthy of giving their all.

Set up a vision for your youth ministry that is an expression of God's dream for the world. When you challenge your youth to change the world for Christ, they will identify with a purpose that is bigger and more compelling than any school, ball team, or club. And it is something that is worthy of their involvement for the rest of their lives.

This is a good place to stop reading and think about your purpose for your youth ministry. Go to the computer now and open the CD-ROM file titled "Foundation." You can print out these two pages and record your thoughts on paper, or you can fill them out on the computer. These questions will help you zero in on how your dream fits in with God's purpose.

Everyone can make a difference. I remember the story of a man and his little boy who would go to the beach together every morning. They were looking for starfish washed up on shore, and, once found, they would throw the helpless creatures back into the surf. One day a huge storm hit, washing millions of starfish onto the beach. The father and son desperately tried to throw all the starfish back before they died.

Another man approached the two and asked what they were doing. "We're just trying to do some good here," they said.

"But you'll never make a difference! All these starfish are dying by the thousands!" said the onlooker.

The little boy stopped and looked at him. Picking up a starfish, he threw it to the waves and said, "I made a difference for *that* one." He picked up another and said, "I made a difference for *that* one . . . and for *that* one . . . and for *that* one . . ." and on and on he went, throwing starfish into the sea, one at a time.

Not only can everyone make a difference, lives are at stake if we don't. God is counting on this generation to make a difference in the world. There are people waiting to be rescued by them!

When you challenge your youth to change the world for Christ, they will identify with a purpose that is bigger and more compelling than any school, ball team, or club.

God is counting on this generation to make a difference in the world. There are people waiting to be rescued by them!

Teaching teens to live and to give. Here in America, we live in one of the richest nations in the world, and it is easy to become a self-centered Christian. We pray for our family, our church, our town, our country, and ourselves. Many people who call themselves Christians are just as selfish as non-Christians. They go to church on Sunday, but are absorbed and preoccupied with the American dream. Ultimately, living to get more "stuff" becomes their priority.

If we will show our teens God's heart for the world, we can teach them a different purpose for living in this prosperous nation. When God calls some to go live overseas and minister full time, others must stay behind and funnel some of the wealth from this great American system into the kingdom of God. It's critical that we do everything we can so that those who are called can get to the nations of the earth.

> "I am never going to get sucked into the American dream and live and pay tithes and die. No! I am going to capitalize on the American system and seize its resources for God's kingdom."

This should be the passion for those called to live here in the States. The Mormons seem more committed to spreading their message than many Christians are in spreading the Truth. May such a thing never be said of the young people who come through your youth ministry.

Instilling in teens a passion for the world teaches them "to live and to give." God wants more than a tithe; He wants tithes, offerings, and the hearts of young people. These teens who stay in the USA may very well get rich, but they will live to give. They are here to start companies and dot-coms and become wealthy so that they can channel money toward the fulfillment of God's vision for the world. Their passion will be: "I have to make an impact on two billion people that have never had a chance!" If we can crank out a generation of people like that, watch out! The world has never seen the impact of a whole generation of Christians focused on God's heart for His world.

The beginning and the end of the foundation. In light of this mandate, what does God want you to do? This is where our plans must begin. We can't begin to dream about the future until we look at the foundation, the bedrock. We must contemplate how we are going to instill kids with this mandate for the rest of their lives. I'm not just saying this because I want people to come on Teen Mania Global Expedition trips. Use any missions group you want. But don't just use them for a summer or short-term trip and be done. Show teens that they can make a difference in the world for the rest of their lives! We want to instill in them a conviction that says:

> *"I have to do something for the world! I need to pray and give like crazy. I have to keep going to the poor and unreached! When I see missionaries come to my church, I am going to bless them like crazy."*

The world has never seen the impact of a whole generation of Christians focused on God's heart for His world.

Start with the end in mind—the purpose— and let that dictate everything else you do.

So the whole purpose for teen Christianity will not be to just stay saved until they die; it will be to make an impact on the world. In light of this mandate, how do we proceed?

Start with the end in mind—the purpose—and let that dictate everything else you do. Again, each of our dreams in ministry will be a little different; but if we all begin to build on this foundation, we will finish with the same goal and direction. When we develop a vision that expresses this mandate, our focus will not be to have the biggest youth group in town or to please the pastor and the parents. We will keep the bigger picture in mind: to nurture a generation of passionate Christ-followers who are committed to blessing the world.

WHAT A GREAT COMMISSION FOUNDATION CAN LOOK LIKE

Even though I love reaching the world and leading a missions organization, I have to keep my missions heart fresh. For that reason, I read missions articles, look at missions videos, and remind myself that there is a world out there.

I remember when I first got turned onto the Lord. I wouldn't even have thought about being a preacher. I thought, "What does God need another preacher for? There are lots of them already." And missionaries—there are lots of them to go around, right? The fact is, *about five percent of all the missionaries in the world work with those two billion who have never had a chance.* This is a tragedy of the highest magnitude.

Our dream for our youth groups is not just to create fun for the sake of activities. We don't want to double our attendance every year to impress. But there is a big world out there that needs to be reached. We need to take kids who are broken and hurting, and put them back together for a purpose—so that they can share their testimonies with the world!

How's this for a testimony? "We had kids on drugs, their families were broken, but now God has restored them. Their families are back together, and God is using these teens to win hundreds or thousands to the Lord." We want to have a small army of young people with testimonies: "I am making a difference in this nation," or "I helped to reach this village that never heard of Christ before," and "I helped to get Bibles into this nation that never had them before."

I believe that God wants leaders who are overcome by His big picture. An imperative part of your dream must be to make teens into world-changers. Ted, an actual successful youth pastor, began his youth ministry with this Great Commission focus. Rather than setting out simply to build a big youth group, he focused on "raising up young people to take the Bible where people don't have one." Everything in his ministry revolved around this. It affected how they organized, planned, and recruited. It's what they told parents and teens. And, sure enough, it's what they did—they raised up kids to be Bible smugglers, and they took Bible-smuggling trips on a regular basis.

With this Great Commission foundation, Ted's youth ministry became the largest in Louisiana with over 1,000 kids. What's the bottom line? They were focused on giving

An imperative part of your dream must be to make teens into world changers.

The vision of the Youth Specialist must be to confront every student with a question that demands a response: "How is your life going to count for the sake of the Great Commission?"

their lives away and changing the world!

Now is the time to think about a people group you would like to reach. Maybe your church has been focusing on a certain nation, or perhpas you're passionate about reaching Muslims, Buddhists, or Hindu people. It's time to make this mission the focus of your youth ministry.

As Youth Specialists, your goal is to get youth seriously plugged into either going or sending for the rest of their lives—not just for a summer. Your training and mentoring before and after short-term summer trips is the glue that makes the lesson stick. You want your teens constantly talking about what happened last summer or what is about to happen this summer.

You want them involved all year with the nations by supporting missionaries and raising money for them or maybe supporting some needy children in another nation. They might raise money to help build an orphanage or help buy a four-wheeler for a missionary who couldn't before find a way to reach a middle-of-nowhere mountain tribe.

You want to build into your students lifelong habits of thinking past themselves to the needs of the world outside their door.

The bedrock purpose of our youth ministries is to make an impact on the world, to reach the world. As a result, the vision of the Youth Specialist must be to confront every student with a question that demands a response: "How is your life going to count for the sake of the Great Commission?"

1. Global Prayer Digest for August 28, 2005, http://www.global-prayer-digest.org/ (accessed October 25, 2005).

2. Larry Caldwell, "Reaching the Really Unreached." BGC World (March, 2002), http://www.bgcworld.org/newstand/standard/stnd0302/10,11.pdf (accessed October 25, 2005).

CHAPTER SIX

Essentials of the Dream

Now that you have begun to dream about all your ministry could and should become, I hope you are filled with a contagious excitement. You are on your way to making a massive impact on this generation! Like the apostle Paul, you're on a path of no regrets that will end someday with the words, "I have finished my course." Each of us longs to hear "well done!" not "well . . . done?" when we meet God face to face. But first, we dream of reaching all those we are supposed to reach!

No one can tell you what your dream should be, but there are some core ingredients that all high-impact youth ministries must contain. (*Notice I call them "youth ministries,"*

We can't get them all single-handedly. So which ones are you going to reach?

and not "youth groups." The word "group" sounds exclusive, rather than a growing and thriving youth ministry!) To discover these essentials, the simpleminded youth leader may call out, "Lord, just tell me what you want me to do. Just write it in the sky or on a tablet." The serious Youth Specialist, on the other hand, asks deep questions that demand answers. God has already deposited within you many aspects of your vision. Now it's time to ask the right questions, questions that will reveal the core ingredients of your ministry.

Getting a clear vision of God's dream is like painting a picture. Remember those paint-by-numbers you did when you were young? At first you had no idea what the picture would look like. But slowly, as you filled in the numbers, the images got clearer. Each one of these questions is like a number in one of those paintings. When you answer the question, the vision will become clearer. Take time to pray over each question as you read on and continue dreaming.

WHO AM I GOING TO REACH?
"Duh . . . I'm going to reach kids!"

Seems at first like a pretty easy question to answer, but take a second look and you'll find that it's a lot more complicated. Before hitting the streets with "reaching young people" as your vague objective, you need to decide *which* ones you are going to pursue. Which type? Most likely, you are excited to reach kids, but if you try to reach them all, you will probably end up reaching very few. None of us can reach them all on our own. I can't reach them all, you can't reach them all, and not a single ministry can reach them all. So we each must define which kids we're going after.

At the Acquire the Fire events I host, we often have guest speakers. Most of the time, we invite speakers who are *not* very much like me. I can reach and touch and minister to certain kids, but I can't get them all. So we invite someone of a different ethnicity or with a different story to share. We can't get them all single-handedly. So which ones are you going to reach?

Reach those who are ready. When deciding whom you are going to reach, follow Jesus' lead. He shared His message first within the church. But when they rejected His teaching, He turned to the broken outside the church; He shared His love with those who realized they needed Him.

What's the lesson in this? *Quit trying to chase the ones that don't want to get caught.* These are often the kids whose parents go to church. You jump through every hoop and do every kind of song, dance, and activity to attract them. In the meantime, there are a lot of hurting kids walking the hallways at school every week, just waiting for someone to show they care.

Don't just reach the ones like you. When thinking about those you are trying to reach, consider the ones who are not like you. If you are a clean-cut middle-class adult, you will naturally attract clean-cut middle-class kids. If you are a surfer-type, then you will probably attract other surfer-types. So if you don't intentionally go after kids who are *not* like you, you probably won't reach them.

There are a lot of hurting kids walking the hallways at school every week, just waiting for someone to show they care.

HUNDREDS HAVE COME!

We bring in about 600-800 youth each [outdoor music] festival. It's a ministry to skater and at-risk teens. A youth church has been started as a result that meets on Sunday nights. Hundreds have come to the Lord!

Praise God!

—Neelka, Youth Specialist

Think about the students in your town. Are they just one big clump of similar people? Of course not! Adults tend to think that all 13–16 year olds are about the same because they are all the same age. But this is a huge mistake! It's like thinking that everyone from a specific country is alike— they all speak the same language, so if we know one of them, we pretty much know them all. What a vast misconception! In reality, every large group of people can be subdivided into smaller groups.

Your teens can help you figure out what these subcultures are. Ask them, "How is your school divided into groups and cliques?" You need to know what they are so you can decide which to address. Which group should you go after?

Marketing groups never go after *everybody*—they know they cannot. So you will see the same potato chip advertised *this* way for one group and *that* way for another group. This is called niche marketing. It's a good model for us to follow because it recognizes a truth—it takes different methods to get different groups to buy the same thing.

So pick your target audience. If you are called to reach the party animals—that's the burden inside of you—then make that group your priority. Designate a large place in your dream for the party animals. Or maybe you realize you must reach girls who are pregnant and unmarried. Whatever your deepest burden, address it in your dream. This is part of what the dreaming process is all about—thinking about which groups are burning in your heart.

HOW DO I REACH MY TARGET AUDIENCE?

After you have decided whom to reach, the next question is obvious: how do I reach this group? This question leads to others (remember at this point to concentrate on the practical):

- *What issues are the kids in this group dealing with?*
- *What interests them?*
- *How can I fill a need in their lives?*
- *What kind of outreach activities do I need to do?*
- *What gifted individuals would I need working beside me in order to effectively reach these kids?*

For example, if your burden is for drug-addicted teens, you will need to recruit leaders who are specially trained to counsel in this area. Maybe you are not an ex-druggie, but you have someone on your team who is, and she is totally on fire for God. Perhaps she would be a great person to help reach a small group or lead an outreach to minister to certain teens.

As you decide how to reach your audience, always work to maximize the leaders that you already have on board.

HOW AM I GOING TO KEEP THEM?

You now know who you are going to reach and how you are going to reach them . . . now you need to ask, "How am I going to keep them?" Perhaps you've figured out what outreach you will do, what type of band you will have, what kind of kids will come in, and how they will all get saved. But if you haven't put any energy into keeping them—in the kingdom and in your youth ministry—you will lose kids. You'll end up wondering why kids keep getting saved but the group doesn't grow. Remember, kids won't stay accidentally—they have to make an intentional choice.

Several subquestions fit here. The simple-minded youth leader would only ask, "How am I going to keep them?" The Youth Specialist asks,

> *Why do I want to keep them? (So they will grow in faith . . . not just so I have a lot of attendees.)*
> *What do I want them to become?*
> *What is my goal for them once they give their lives to Jesus? Is it just to be good church-going folk the rest of their lives?*
> *Where do I want to take them in their walk with God?*
> *How do I want them to grow once they are committed to Him?*

Pizza parties and lock-ins won't keep them coming, but the answers to these questions will.

HOW MANY COULD WE REALLY REACH?

As a Youth Specialist, you need to dream about how big this thing could really get. When you talk about numbers, it's because you're thinking about the *kids* you want to reach. After all, each number represents a living soul—we're not in the math business; we're in the soul business! When people say, "You're only in this for numbers," don't worry—you know that numbers equal people.

Have the courage to dream a little bit about numbers! Your energy will skyrocket when you start thinking, "Wow! We really *could* have 100 or 200 or even 300 kids in our group! It has never been done in the history of our town, but we could do this!"

One of the first-ever Teen Mania rallies was in Erie, Kansas. I hadn't intended Teen Mania to become a whole ministry; it was just something I was doing while in college. I couldn't stand just going to class—I wanted to reach out and see people get saved. So we did an outreach for some young people. We planned on going into a little town and thought the name "Teen Mania" might just create enough curiosity to get young people to come. One month in advance, we put big banners across the street all over this two-horse town. The banners read, "Teen Mania is coming! Get ready!" We hung up posters and passed out bumper stickers to all the high school kids. Curiosity grew.

When the day of the event came, we had *more kids at the event than the entire population of the town of Erie*. Teens flooded us from outlying towns. They were listening to the bands and getting saved!

When you think big, there is a tangible excitement that fuels your heart. People will catch your enthusiasm when you dream bigger than they've ever imagined. Think about how big it could get by the end of one year or two years. Dare to step out and do something that has never been done in your town before. This is how revolutions are started!

WHAT ARE THE REAL NEEDS OF THE TEENS I WANT TO REACH?

What needs are not being fulfilled for youth today? Many statistics and surveys show that kids in our society are very relationship-driven right now. Maybe it is the vacuum caused by their moms and dads working all the time.

As a Youth Specialist, you need to dream about how big this thing could really get.

Dare to step out and do something that has never been done in your town before. This is how revolutions are started!

Maybe it's the hole created by divorce. Maybe it's addictive Internet use. Statistics show that there is a direct correlation between the amount of time kids spend on the Internet and the degree of loneliness they feel. Imagine what will happen as Internet use increases more and more. Forty-eight percent of kids already use the Internet on a regular basis, and the numbers continue to rise.[1]

Some needs are felt needs, meaning kids know they need help in a certain area (for example, they are lonely or depressed or pregnant). Other needs are real issues that they don't even know they need help with. Kids with these unfelt needs are like children who need vitamins and don't know it, so their parents have to find a clever way to get them to take the pills. We must consider how we are going to address those needs, whether felt or unfelt. We need to show youth that the Bible is the answer to those needs, and not just a "spiritual, but irrelevant document."

A huge need for this generation is the need for a father. You will have teens who don't know their dads or have divorced parents. You must understand that we can't just be big brothers or happy-go-lucky youth guys. These kids need a godly authority figure in their lives. That goes for both guys and girls.

We know what happens to a girl who doesn't get enough attention from her father: she tries to get attention from guys in other ways. So if you give her fatherly, godly attention, suddenly she realizes she doesn't need the false attention of boyfriends. By understanding the needs of those you intend to reach and how you will meet those needs with the ministry team you assemble, you will begin to attract those very students to your ministry.

WHAT IS THE NATURE AND CHARACTER OF THE GROUP THAT I AM TO LEAD?

The size of your group in the future is only part of the dream. There are many groups that grow in numbers but never become anything more than a fun "Jesus rally" with no solid disciples. You need to decide what is to be the nature of your group. You may think, "Well, the group's nature will be determined by the dynamic and personality of the kids who form the group." Not so. It will be determined by whatever you allow or train them to be.

Ask yourself, what kind of Christians do I want these kids to become? Let's say you want the personality of your group to be distinguished by the fact that these students really love to worship God with all their hearts. Start to imagine what your Wednesday night meeting should look and feel like in order to grow an army of worshipers. What would have to be there in order to inspire them to worship like that? A band? PA system? Lights? A real worship team?

If they are the best worshipers in the whole church, then everyone else in the church will realize that these kids really love God.

What other words would you want to use to describe your youth ministry? Do you want them to be soul winners? Then the question, "How do I turn these kids into a

By understanding the needs of those you intend to reach and how you will meet those needs with the ministry team you assemble, you will begin to attract those very students to your ministry.

Whether it is sending some kids or supporting other missionaries, reaching the world must be a priority of every Youth Specialist.

group that will bring people to the Lord?" ought to plague you until it is answered. Set a goal to instill in them a passion to reach out to others as a natural part of their lives and they won't be ashamed or afraid to win people for the Lord. Remember, this means more than just a once-a-year sermon on how they need to win souls and then hoping they do it. This could mean that in addition to training, you take them with you to go out and win souls. If you want to turn them into "soul winners," you need to *define what that is in your mind and determine how you will accomplish it.*

The important thing to remember here is that you, as leader, need to develop a clear picture of what you want the personality of the group to be, and then you must engineer your group to become that. We must help them develop into people who have: *respect, self-control, honor for their parents, love for purity, hate for sin, discernment about the lies of the world. They must become disciples and disciple others.* These are just a few of the essentials.

HOW WILL I MEASURE THEIR SPIRITUAL GROWTH?

I would encourage you to think about how you can measure the growth in your teens' spirituality. This is not done very often. Many Christians don't know that they are supposed to grow, or in what areas they should grow. Research shows that most Christians feel they stop growing after their first two years in the church.

So many times we just tell our groups to keep reading their Bibles, praying, and coming to youth group, but we fail to intentionally disciple them. If you have some serious God-followers, they are going to want spiritual food so they can grow. If we don't do that, they will starve to death under your supervision! No wonder your teens get bored and walk away from their commitment to Christ.

There ought to be some benchmarks of growth in your church. Benchmarks might include: how much time they are spending with God, how much of the Bible they are reading each year, character traits that they are really developing, sin that they are overcoming, how many books that they have read about walking closer to the Lord or devotional types of books, etc. Think about how you will chart the growth of these God-followers and how you are going to be able to tell they are growing. This is imperative for a Youth Specialist. Teens need to see they are on track as soon as they commit to the Lord.

It is like joining the military. Everyone knows that if you enlist as a private, there are a lot of ranks you can progress to. It is inherent to the process. NO one wants to stay at a private E1 status. In fact, if after 20 years in the army you were still an E1 you would be a laughingstock!

WHAT ALL THE BUZZ IS

[I had] eight to ten kids, mostly skeptics and "fringe players." Only about two of them were really committed Christians. Now I have 20 very energetic young Christian teens, and they are constantly bringing in new kids to see what all the buzz is about.

—Denny, Youth Specialist

Our problem has been that we beg teens
to come each week, but don't give
them the substance needed
to really belong.

Yet it seems we have plenty of E1 Christians in our pews today.

So as part of your dream, think of how you will track teen growth and what track you're going to give them to run on so that *they can see* that they have grown in Christ.

HOW WILL I POINT THEM TOWARD THE GREAT COMMISSION?

As we discussed in the last chapter, I am quite confident that any wise leader's dream is going to include missions because that is the most important thing on God's heart. Are we raising up a generation so that they can do something to dramatically affect this world? What does that look like? Well, it could mean having a youth group missions trip every year, *and* sending two or three kids from your group on a longer trip every year as well. Truthfully, I am not trying to advertise Teen Mania's Global Expeditions. This is about raising up kids that care about the world because it is so easy to be an American and be self-centered and only think about your youth group and your town and your country.

God needs the whole Body of Christ to be thinking about the rest of the world. And as we talked about earlier, we get the chance to set the pace for the next generation of Christians. So whatever we breathe into them as imperative, is what they will think is most important. So, how do missions connect to your youth ministry? Whether it is sending some kids or supporting other missionaries, reaching the world must be a priority of every Youth Specialist.

WHAT IS THE IDENTITY OF YOUR GROUP?

Ask any teen, "What are you into?" and they will tell you about the activities in their lives that they feel are most important. Whatever they say to you is where they find their identity. Some will say, "I'm into sports, or a certain band, or friends, or school." Realize that their first comments are what they feel "a part of." Even Christian teens—when you ask them that question—will say "drama, school, sports, or choir." They come to church, but their identity and center of their lives are found elsewhere.

One of the reasons that youth have a hard time coming to youth group each week or to your special events is because they feel more a part of something else than your youth ministry. For example, when you tell them your group is doing something exciting, they are noncommittal until they figure out if they have a ball game or other activity *more important to them.*

I dream of the day that a coach says to his team at school they have practices and games, but the student says, "Well, I need to check my youth ministry calendar to make sure I can fit in my practices!" Kids are so committed to these other things because it's where they find their identity. They *go* to church and they *go* to youth group, but their *identity* is with their ball team.

So one of the most important reasons to dream is to figure out what the vision is and where the group is going so

Teens don't want to just come to a meeting, they want to belong to a vision.

that kids understand this is who we are and *this is what we are about*. When teens understand that, then they can decide if they want to be a part of it. Our problem has been that we beg teens to come each week, but don't give them the substance needed to really belong. Teens don't want to just come to a meeting, *they want to belong to a vision!*

Here are some practical elements of teen ministry that will help clarify the identity of your group.

Identity requires a name. Part of a team's identity is a name and mascot. I would encourage you to have a name for your youth group or ministry. Don't just call yourself "the youth group of whatever church" because that is just an add-on. School sports don't just call themselves the "football team at Hennery High," they call themselves by name, the name of the mascot. The name, like *180* or *Crossfire*, can be something unique that you invent, or you can vote on it. (I don't normally encourage voting on many things, but a name is an okay thing to vote on.) You could have a contest and the one who thinks of the name that YOU choose wins something great.

Identity is easier with a symbol. Another thing to consider when creating identity is a symbol or logo. Even the early Christians had a logo. They drew a fish to represent their leader, Jesus Christ. Think about artwork for a few minutes. We live in a society that likes flashy things, which is why advertising works. Our product is a billion times better than anything the world can offer, but if we never get the kids' attention, they will never know about the product. Kids are used to seeing things and receiving information through a cool brochure or video clip, and we need to communicate our vision in a way that is clear to them. Sure, we can sit back, leave it boring, and hope they will come, but the fact is, *if you don't use the right bait, you won't catch the fish.*

So what kind of artwork do you need? Maybe some

type of brochure or flyer that talks about your ministry. It should appeal to both Christian and non-Christian. Another piece, or even the same piece, could appeal to adults inside and outside of the church, explaining what you are doing to help teens. What would that look like? This is not the kind of flier that you need really quick, so you run something off the Xerox machine, and it's crooked. Design something exciting, attractive, and timeless that you can use for the next year for both kids and adults. You don't want to have to print a new concept every time you need something. I know some youth groups have printed small, four-color invitations that fold out. Kids take them to school and pass them out to all of their friends, and they use them all year long. Even dreaming big we should still be wise stewards with our resources. A lot of the cost of printing is the setup of the press. To run 1,000 extra copies is really cheap. It's doing the artwork setup that's expensive. And there are many teens who can do artwork on their computers for you; ask them to help and to give ideas that THEY think are cool.

Identity requires a place. Part of the identity of your group will come from a name and a symbol, and part will come from a youth facility. If you do not have a youth room or a youth facility, I would encourage you to find a way to pray one in. Part of dreaming is to forget what money is needed and not let it harness your vision. Teens need to walk in and *like* to be there—not be embarrassed to bring their friends. Where teens hang out is part of their identity. We want them to feel like part of a team, its dream, and its place.

If you don't make room for teen leaders, they will never rise up.

If you don't know how to decorate, ask someone. You could decorate your space like a bedroom (without all the clothes on the floor). Create a place where they'll feel comfortable and want to be. Marketers have done research and found that there is a globalized youth culture now. The bedrooms of teenagers all around the world look the same: same posters, same heroes, music, sports; all are almost identical. So it shouldn't be too hard to figure out how to decorate. It should make your teens feel comfortable. In your youth facility, you are going to want to think about:

- *How big should the space be, and what color?*
- *Should it have lights?*
- *What functions does it need to fill?*
- *Should it have video screens?*

Forget about the money, and think about the dream. If Jesus were the youth pastor trying to reach these kids, what would the room look like? What would it be? What *could* it be?

Identity requires a specific service. Part of the identity of your group is the kind of service you have. Imagine holding the most amazing, Spirit-filled, saving-people-in-masses service; what would that look like?

- *What would the worship be like?*
- *What would the preaching be like?*
- *Would there be altar calls?*
- *What would object lessons be like?*
- *Could kids be leading others to get saved during the service?*
- *Could young people be hanging out in the back so struggling teens would have peers to talk to?*

- *Could young people be a part of actually presenting and doing dramas up front to go along with your message?*
- *Would you have handouts that go with your sermon for kids to take notes on?*
- *What about teenage leaders?*

HOW WILL I RAISE UP TEEN LEADERS?

Every highly productive youth ministry will raise up teen leaders. What are you going to do to develop those leaders? The fact is, you already have too much to do, especially as you start to dream bigger. You can't do it all yourself. If you could do it by yourself, then you wouldn't be dreaming big enough. So how will you recruit them, how will you develop them, what jobs will you give them? Make room in your system for teen leaders. If you don't make room for teen leaders, they will never rise up.

HOW WILL I ENGAGE ADULT VOLUNTEERS?

Another essential of any world-class dream is adult volunteers. More than just parents helping out on a week-end, these adults are committed to moving your vision forward. What specific role do adult volunteers play? How many will you need? Your dream is going to require many of them. How will you get the ideal people? How do you make sure the adults who come are the right ones?

We'll address this issue of raising up teen and adult leaders more fully in a later chapter.

HOW WILL I USE NEW MEDIA?

Since we live in the new millennium, you need to be thinking about where TV, radio, and the Internet will play a part in your vision. Instead of just meeting every Wednesday, how can you connect with youth every day? This is a media-driven generation. Studies show that on

If we are only there for kids once a week on Wednesday nights, we will be irrelevant to their lives.

average, people see 30,000 messages each day coaxing them to buy this, try this, do this, etc. If we are only there for kids once a week on Wednesday nights, we will be irrelevant to their lives and will not connect with them. Jesus connected with people. He used object lessons out of everyday life to connect. He pointed to lilies as an example of God's provision for clothes. He looked at the birds of the air and used them to teach God's loving provision for all of our needs. To fishermen He talked about fishing, to farmers He talked about a sower and the seed. He helped people understand spiritual truths using things they were familiar with. We need to do the same thing.

As we talk about the Internet, TV, radio, and other media, we need to think about how to make it work for us in the 21st century to communicate truth to kids. Maybe you've never thought about having a weekly television program on a local TV station, but you need to. You need to dream about it. I know that there are many Youth Specialists reading this right now who could have a weekly television program, reaching out to people in the area and almost for free. You can't even imagine now how to get it, but you *could*. Think about how you could "expand your tent pegs."

Using the Internet, local radio, and other forms of media or what is called now the "new media" is a way to be where the teens are living. I know some youth pastors who run quick, thought-provoking, one-minute ads on the local secular stations. I remember when I first had an opportunity to do TV programs for teens, I thought it was crazy. I had never seen myself as a televangelist and I wanted nothing to do with TV. I was offered a regular national TV program for free and even then I was not sure I was interested. The Lord dealt with my heart about dreaming a little bigger. How are we going to reach all the young people that must be touched if we do not use the airwaves? If we don't seize the airwaves and Internet, we are letting the enemy grab all the teens' attention. It was over 10 years ago that I started using TV, and I cannot tell you how many lives have been changed! I have heard stories of teens who were ready to commit suicide, but saw the program and stopped, gave their lives to Jesus, and are now making a huge difference for God! Find out how God wants to use the media in your dream (even if it is as simple as a Web page for your youth ministry so your kids can stay updated).

HOW WILL I INVOLVE THE PARENTS OF MY TEENS?

Your dream needs to include how you are going to engage the parents of your teens. You need to make them feel a part of what you are doing with their kids. Pull them into the vision. Meet with them regularly. Give them the notes on your sermon topic for next month. Give them tools to hold their kids accountable. Give them tips for parenting. Give your parents' group a name if you want . . . for example, a youth ministry I know calls themselves "Warriors." The parents are called "Parents of Warriors," or "POW." Whatever you do, don't overlook your parents.

Find out how God wants to use the media in your dream.

How are we going to reach all the young people that might be touched if we do not use the airwaves?

HOW WILL I CAPTURE THE HEART OF MY PASTOR AND LAYPEOPLE?

Part of your dream should cover how you are going to keep your pastor and laypeople engaged. You don't want to be doing this vision in another time warp. You need your pastor to be your biggest cheerleader. You need all the laypeople praying for you, giving large offerings to all the initiatives you are dreaming of, and volunteering to help. You must think of all the ways you will keep them informed of what's going on. You want to give them more than just information, you want to make part of your mission *to get them to love teens just as much as you do.* This is not one sermon, or one video clip. This is regular face time with them in front of the church, handouts, and finding ways for the group of teens to regularly serve the lay-people. You want to be very visible.

One practical thing you can do is to have the adults in your church go through the *Battle Cry for a Generation* book and study guide. (Go to **www.acquirethefire.com** and look under resources to order the book.) This will shock them and open their hearts for the battle for a young generation. It will help them to see how they can be part of the answer. The study guide encourages accountability and can be a strategic tool to get the whole congregation on your side. Make it an aim to get 10 percent, then 20 percent, then 50 percent of your church to go through it, so you will have an army of church members who are fully engaged in helping you to rescue a generation and find a way to plug into your vision.

AT THE END OF MY LIFE, WHAT WOULD I FEEL TERRIBLE ABOUT LEAVING UNDONE?

This is a little broader question. When you consider your dream, what is the one thing—if I never do it—that will make me feel like I totally blew it. One of the ways that God speaks to us is through convictions. He puts a conviction inside of you that you have to reach a certain group of kids, and if you don't live up to that thing you will feel like you have failed. Identify some of those convictions. For example, it might be "If I don't start an outreach for the down-and-out kids, whatever it may be, I'll feel terrible." Identify what are some of the convictions by asking yourself, *if I don't do them, how will I feel at the end of my life?* Terrible? Then you better do that thing.

There is a difference between *good ideas* and *"must-haves."* In your dream you will have a lot of great ideas; you will also have some you know you must do. Make a list and ask the Lord to help you define how much of it is must-do and which part of it is *a pretty good idea.* Which is good, and which is God?

When Katie and I started we felt a conviction to reach out to young people but I also felt a conviction to reach the people of the world through missions. I was frustrated because I didn't know how it could all happen. Sometimes you have to wrestle with God like Jacob did. Too many of us spend a total of five minutes daydreaming, asking God to handle it, and then we can't figure out why it doesn't

God will breathe His dreams into your heart and then you will go and walk those things out; this is the adventurous life of a Youth Specialist!

Just because God's behind a vision doesn't mean He doesn't want you to do the grunt work.

happen. Instead, you need to wrestle and pray and wrestle and pray for an understanding for priorities. We are talking about your destiny here, the reason you were born. We are talking about reaching a generation here. Surely it is worth wrestling over for a season!

I remember talking to Rich Mullins about his song "Awesome God." I asked him how he wrote that song. I assumed he had a great quiet time and there he was with God and his Bible and he was in worship, maybe with a piano, and God just spoke and glory filled the room and it was awesome. I wanted to know what happened and how God spoke to him. After thinking he said, "It was just a lot of hard work." At the time, I thought that was kind of unspiritual, but it isn't. Isn't it interesting that *something that takes a lot of hard work ends up being incredibly anointed?* So it will be with your dream. Just because you are working hard on it, does not mean you are trying to do it in the flesh. Now a whole generation has sung Rich's song in worship and it's become a classic.

Just because God's behind a vision doesn't mean He doesn't want you to do the grunt work. God wants to *know how bad you want it*, how hard you are willing to work, how hungry you are, etc. Will you pray and stay on your face?

Before we started Teen Mania, I had to wrestle with God about young people, missions, and how the two could possibly be connected. Finally I told Him I would get on the floor right there in my little loft area on my knees and I was not moving until I heard from Him. I decided that I was not going to go through my whole life wishing I had done something else. I could not figure out how these two could go together. I didn't want to go get another "job"—tread water for a while—then hope to do the dream He'd called me to later. And there is something about that level of seriousness that lets God say, "Okay, now you are ready to hear." That is when He breathed into me the dream of Teen Mania. It had never occurred to me before, but He wanted us *to raise up an army of young people to love God like crazy and give them a chance to go and change the world.*

We need a generation of leaders who are dreamers that won't be stopped, no matter what. If we don't dream it first, there is no way we will do it. What a tragedy for us to hold God's hand back from what He wants to do with young people all because we dare not dream big enough.

I would encourage you to do what Mary did in Luke 2:19 when the angel Gabriel told her she would be pregnant: Mary cherished these things and treasured them up in her heart.

Some of the things that God wishes for you, you are just going to have to cherish them between you and God. Keep reminding Him that you know it's in there and that He spoke it to you. Other people may still not understand, but you and God cherish your dreams together. Don't start proclaiming parts of your dream

from the mountaintops yet. As your dream matures, there is a very clear and diplomatic and well-thought-through way

If we don't dream it first, there is no way we will do it.

to introduce your dream to people that will make them want to participate. Later, we'll spend time developing and refining and putting some teeth to your dream.

I encourage you to start the dreaming process. Write down everything that comes to your mind, crossing out things that do not really matter, things that are nice to have but are not imperative. Begin to do this and you are on your way to stepping into a whole new realm of life. God will breathe His dreams into your heart and then you will go and walk those things out; this is the adventurous life of a Youth Specialist!

I want to encourage you to build some time into your schedule to look at your dream again and begin to refine it. Go back to your computer now and open the CD-ROM file titled "Find Your Dream." Take all the time you need to build your vision here. This is important; don't let anything interrupt you. We cannot continue doing the same thing we have always done. We cannot get consumed with lots of "youth ministry activities" that have no purpose.

God's way of advancing His kingdom is putting a dream in the heart of His leaders, and bringing people alongside to help implement that dream. Now go be that leader!

1. Daniel L. Weiss, "The Online Life of Teenagers," Citizen Link, Focus on Social Issues (August 11, 2005),http://www.family.org/cforum/fosi/pornography/facts/a0026839.cfm (accessed October 26, 2005).

CHAPTER SEVEN

Bold Pursuit of the Dream

The sad fact is that too many youth pastors (and pastors, for that matter) do not have a dream. They plod on day after day struggling to stay a step ahead of what they will preach next week. Dreaming is work and quickly makes us weary. Yet without one, we find ourselves pedaling faster and faster just to keep up. In time, we burn out (maybe this is a reason for so much turnover among youth workers). Then we either get out of the ministry or we complain, "Man, that pastor worked me too hard!"

Since you are still reading this, I am confident that this doesn't describe you and, hopefully, you're doing the dreaming exercises. Now that you have tapped into God's

Prepare yourself for some opposition.

big vision for your life and youth ministry, what comes next? Well, prepare yourself for some opposition. Once a Youth Specialist starts seeking God's *big, far-reaching, and amazing* vision, the devil lines up troops for battle. Why? He has had a stronghold on this generation for a long time and suddenly you have drawn them to the kingdom of God. Now you're treading in his territory. Do you think the devil will take this lying down?

Look at the example of Daniel's story. He set out to follow God more closely, and an angel explained to him what happened when he set this godly course:

> *"Do not be afraid, Daniel. Since the first day that you set your mind to gain understanding and to humble yourself before your God, your words were heard, and I have come in response to them. But the prince of the Persian kingdom resisted me twenty-one days. Then Michael, one of the chief princes, came to help me, because I was detained there with the king of Persia."*
> —Daniel 10:12–13

When one of you steps up to be a general in this battle for our youth, your resolve is known immediately in heaven. And just as quickly, the devil responds by sending his generals to oppose you on the spiritual front.

Opposition may also come from within—people may dismiss you as just a dreamer. I often heard that in the early days of Teen Mania, and I still hear it in some circles today. People refuse to believe how many kids are willing to take their faith seriously and how many kids we can attract to conventions or send on missions.

Whether from the enemy without or doubters within,

do expect opposition. *Don't* expect it will be a walk in the park. How, then, do you boldly overcome opposition? Let's look at Joshua's example of leadership.

JOSHUA'S BOLDNESS

Boldness comes from a gut-level conviction that your dream is a mandate from God. It's not just a whim or man-made hope. When you encounter opposition you need to be certain that *this is from the heart of God, this is right, this is real, and this is where we are supposed to go.*

You will recall that Moses too had a dream from God which he shared with the Israelites—the promised land. He sent 12 men to spy out the land and 10 of them ridiculed the dream: it was too dangerous—after all, there were giants! As a result of their lack of faith and boldness, not one of those guys entered the promised land. After Moses' death, Joshua took over the leadership of Israel. You could call him the next youth minister! He did not shrink from fearlessly leading his group to possess the land.

Wherever you step out. What was the dream? Joshua was only promised the land that he stepped on. He had to go forward in faith.

> *I will give you every place where you set your foot, as I promised Moses. Your territory will extend from the*

When one of you steps up to be a general in this battle for our youth, your resolve is known immediately in heaven. And just as quickly, the devil responds by sending his generals to oppose you on the spiritual front.

Just because you have a huge dream doesn't mean that you don't have a reason to be terrified!

desert to Lebanon, and from the great river, the Euphrates—all the Hittite country—to the Great Sea on the west. No one will be able to stand up against you all the days of your life. As I was with Moses, so I will be with you; I will never leave you nor forsake you.
—Joshua 1:3–5

The proper frame of mind. In verse 6, God tells Joshua, "Be strong and courageous." In verse 7, He says, "Be strong and very courageous." Verse 9: "Be strong and courageous. Do not be terrified; do not be discouraged, for the LORD your God will be with you wherever you go."

Are you starting to see a pattern? *Be strong and courageous.* It is one thing for God to repeat Himself once, but three or four times? Obviously, it was important to reassure Joshua. Did Joshua have a reason to be terrified? Of course he did. This was a land of giants!

Just because you have a huge dream doesn't mean that you don't have a reason to be terrified! Huge dreams are formidable. You want four-color brochures instead of Xerox copies; that's huge! You want buses and vans, video projectors, and your own local television program on every night of the week! All this looks as daunting as a whole tribe of giants!

I want you to pay attention to something here. God wasn't merely comforting Joshua. He wasn't saying, "Oh, Joshua, I just want to encourage you; you can do it!" No, He said, "Be strong, I am commanding you!" This was not an option; it was a *choice God expected Joshua to make.* In other words, even when you don't feel like it, you'd better be strong, and you'd better be courageous! Why? "Because I am counting on you, Joshua. These people are counting on you. There is a dream and a vision and unless you are bold and courageous, it will not happen." God was counting on His man to be bold so the dream could be fulfilled.

A giant step of faith and boldness. Years ago when Teen Mania first moved to Texas, we had been at our headquarters in Tulsa for 10 years renting different offices. When we outgrew one, we would rent another. We owned a couple of vans, but never anything of great value. I would look at churches with big buildings and marvel at the cost and fundraising involved.

Then God put the idea of a permanent headquarters into my heart. I realized we were wasting a lot of money renting things. This was most obvious at a hotel in Miami. Every year we'd pay them a lot of money to stay with them, and then the next year we'd come back and they had renovated their lobby. We began to think that we had a ministry of renovating hotel lobbies all over Miami. I knew it would be much better stewardship to build a place for the kingdom of God where kids could get trained. So we began to search the country and finally found a suitable place in Garden Valley, Texas. But it cost over a million dollars! How do you raise a million dollars in youth ministry? It was overwhelming.

The tragedy is that too many look at the giants and miss God standing big behind them. The truth is, *if there are no giants in your dream, your dream is not big enough.* God has never called us to do something that is *possible.* God wants to do it, not you. Know your dream and be courageous about it. Don't let the giants intimidate you!

Put your foot in the water! Joshua had an unshakable conviction—"If God is for us, who can be against us?"

The tragedy is that too many look at the giants and miss God standing big behind them.

Imagine Joshua that day they marched in to take possession of the promised land. He ordered the priests with the ark of the covenant to march to the edge of the river and *put their feet in the water.* They didn't yell to God, "Roll back the river first! Then we will walk through!" They put their feet in the water first, *and then* the river rolled back. Do you have that kind of faith? Be daring enough to say that you're going to double or triple the size of your youth group and change the world! If you don't have the faith to step out into the water, it will never roll back.

Roll up your sleeves and get busy. Here is the other side of that coin. Many people, once they conceive their dream, sit back and wait for the Lord to make it happen. They're so convinced He'll step in that they take no action themselves. Well, maybe He's waiting for you!

God's plan is to partner with mankind. He is the source of all power, but *He does it with us,* not without us. Your job is not to sit idly by and wait for God to do something great while your dreams flounder and go unrealized. It's to roll up your sleeves, pick up the task, and labor alongside God to bring those dreams to fruition. Get your hands dirty!

Too many people simply talk about the great plans they have for the future. These people will likely fail to touch the people they were meant to reach. Do you know why? Because they were not willing to sweat.

Remember the command that Moses the servant of the Lord gave you: "The Lord your God is giving you rest and has granted you this land. Your wives, your children and your livestock may stay in the land that Moses gave you east of the Jordan, but all your fighting men, fully armed, must cross over ahead of your brothers. You are to help your brothers until the Lord gives them rest, as he has done for you, and until they too have taken possession of the land that the Lord your God is giving them."

—Joshua 1:13–15

The divine partnership. Isn't that interesting? Scripture says, "Until they too have taken possession of the land that the LORD your God is giving them." It sounds like an oxymoron. They are *taking possession* but *God is giving it to them.* In other words, they didn't just walk in and the armies fell down; they had to fight and take it.

Roll up your sleeves! If you want your dream, you'd better be willing to fight for it. Get ready to sweat! You may even bleed a little bit. You're not involved with youth ministry because you want a vacation. I know that most of you are already sweating and caring and staying up late nights with kids. You're willing to work.

So get ready to work. Don't sit around waiting for God to make a miracle. Partnership with God means accepting the dream He gives you, and going after it with all your strength.

Jesus displayed the same picture of partnership. This partnership can be seen in Jesus' ministry as well. When Jesus fed the crowd of 5,000, He made His disciples do all the footwork. Jesus told them to seat the crowd in groups of 50 (I'm sure they felt very honored to get that job), and He told them to distribute loaves and fish to everyone.

God's plan is to partner with mankind.

Partnership with God means accepting the dream He gives you, and going after it with all your strength.

After the picnic, Jesus told them to clean up the leftovers as well. That's when they realized they had played a part in Jesus' miracle.

Here's the point. Couldn't Jesus just have rained fish and loaves right down into the crowd's hands? He is, after all, the Son of God. He could have saved the disciples a lot of work. Instead He chose to use *their sweat and labor to accomplish the miracle*. God doesn't want to do the work alone; He wants to partner with us.

Little by little. Moses described to the Israelites what would happen when they went into the promised land:

> When the LORD your God brings you into the land you are entering to possess and drives out before you many nations—the Hittites, Girgashites, Amorites, Canaanites, Perizzites, Hivites and Jebusites, seven nations larger and stronger than you—and when the LORD your God has delivered them over to you and you have defeated them, then you must destroy them totally.
> —Deuteronomy 7:1–2

Here's that same paradox again: the Lord will *deliver them to you* but *you still have to defeat them*. He is delivering, but we are defeating. It's still a partnership thing.

Look at another truth that comes out a few verses later:

> The Lord your God will drive out those nations before you, little by little. You will not be allowed to eliminate

them all at once, or the wild animals will multiply around you. But the Lord your God will deliver them over to you, throwing them into great confusion until they are destroyed.

—Deuteronomy 7:22–23

He is speaking of *persistence*. Notice it says "little by little." The Israelites were very excited about the dream of entering the promised land—they had been waiting for 40 years! But here God warns them it isn't going to happen overnight. How often do we receive a vision, work hard at it for three weeks, then decide that it wasn't God after all and give up? Then a month later we get excited about something else only to abandon that dream when it doesn't come to pass right away.

If a dream is really from God, we need to set our faces like flint and realize that we are going to have to knock down doors, endure some discomfort, and persevere until the job is done! Resist the feeling of frustration when you don't accomplish your goals at once! God knows what He is doing. If you went in and took the whole land at once, unseen wild animals may gather round and devour you and your flock. God's timing is perfect.

If God withholds part of our dream, we can trust that it is for our own good. I remember many times when, if we could have seen the entire scope of His plan, we would have been too intimidated to take a step forward! Our decision to move ahead with the purchase of the property for a big campus was one of those times.

The property needed some work—it didn't have enough buildings, the dorm was barely big enough for the interns, and the office needed to be gutted. It wasn't everything we thought we needed, but it was enough. So, in faith, we made a down payment on the $1 million and moved in. Quickly, we began to raise money to develop and expand the facilities. Once again, God showed up and

If a dream is really from God, we need to set our faces like flint and realize that we are going to have to knock down doors, endure some discomfort, and persevere until the job is done!

did more than anything we could have imagined in "our plan." Now, nine years later, we have put nearly $30 million into the grounds.

The point of this story is that if God had revealed all the details of His plan for our headquarters right at the start, it would have been too overwhelming. We would have said no way and headed in a different direction. But when God fills in His vision little by little, it "chases out the wild animals" and makes it less intimidating. (Actually, we had to literally drive out wild animals too! There were red ants everywhere!) So, be willing to let your dream fill in little by little. Make the most strategic use of each step of the way.

That is exactly what the next book will help you accomplish. It's time to plan!